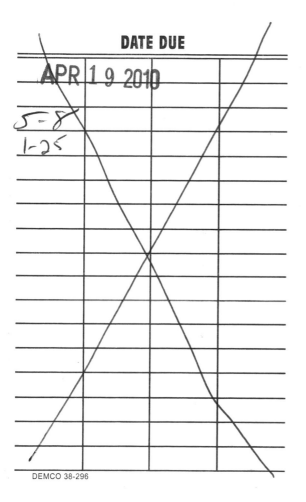

DATE DUE

APR 1 9 2010

5-8
1-25

DEMCO 38-296

BEYONCÉ KNOWLES

BEYONCÉ KNOWLES

A Biography

Janice Arenofsky

GREENWOOD BIOGRAPHIES

GREENWOOD PRESS
WESTPORT, CONNECTICUT • LONDON

3/5/10

Library of Congress Cataloging-in-Publication Data

Arenofsky, Janice.
  Beyoncé Knowles : a biography / Janice Arenofsky.
    p. cm. — (Greenwood biographies, ISSN 1540–4900)
  Includes bibliographical references and index.
  ISBN 978–0–313–35914–9 (alk. paper)
  1. Beyoncé, 1981–   2. Rhythm and blues musicians—United States—Biography.
3. Singers—United States—Biography.   I. Title.
  ML420.K675A87   2009
  782.42164092—dc22
  [B]   2009010349

British Library Cataloguing in Publication Data is available.

Library of Congress Catalog Card Number: 2009010349

ISBN: 978–0–313–35914–9
ISSN: 1540–4900

First published in 2009

Greenwood Press, 88 Post Road West, Westport, CT 06881
An imprint of Greenwood Publishing Group, Inc.
www.greenwood.com

Printed in the United States of America

∞™

The paper used in this book complies with the
Permanent Paper Standard issued by the National
Information Standards Organization (Z39.48–1984).

10 9 8 7 6 5 4 3 2 1

CONTENTS

CONTENTS

Photo essay begins after page 94

SERIES FOREWORD

In response to high school and public library needs, Greenwood developed this distinguished series of full-length biographies specifically for student use. Prepared by field experts and professionals, these engaging biographies are tailored for high school students who need challenging yet accessible biographies. Ideal for secondary school assignments, the length, format and subject areas are designed to meet educators' requirements and students' interests.

Greenwood offers an extensive selection of biographies spanning all curriculum-related subject areas including social studies, the sciences, literature and the arts, history and politics, as well as popular culture, covering public figures and famous personalities from all time periods and backgrounds, both historical and contemporary, who have made an impact on American and/or world culture. Greenwood biographies were chosen based on comprehensive feedback from librarians and educators. Consideration was given to both curriculum relevance and inherent interest. The result is an intriguing mix of the well known and the unexpected, the saints and sinners from long-ago history and contemporary pop culture. Readers will find a wide array of subject choices from fascinating crime figures like Al Capone to inspiring pioneers like Margaret Mead, from the greatest minds of our time like Stephen Hawking to the most amazing success stories of our day like J. K. Rowling.

While the emphasis is on fact, not glorification, the books are meant to be fun to read. Each volume provides in-depth information about the subject's life from birth through childhood, the teen years, and adulthood.

A thorough account relates family background and education, traces personal and professional influences, and explores struggles, accomplishments, and contributions. A timeline highlights the most significant life events against a historical perspective. Bibliographies supplement the reference value of each volume.

INTRODUCTION

"B," as Beyoncé Knowles is known by her friends, burst onto the national stage in 1992, when the tween-aged vocalist-dancer and the girl group, Girl's Tyme, appeared on the television talent program *Star Search*. Like Jennifer Hudson, who debuted on TV's "American Idol" and with whom Beyoncé co-starred in the 2006 movie *Dreamgirls*, Girl's Tyme failed to make the judges' cut.

Nevertheless, it was a defining moment for the musically gifted grade-schooler from Houston, Texas. Although Beyoncé was devastated at the loss, she did not give up. Instead, the R&B performer fashioned a silk purse from a sow's ear and turned a negative into a positive with support from her family and her faith.

Four years later, Columbia Records signed the group (now renamed Destiny's Child) to a recording contract. As lead singer, Beyoncé supplied the focus and motivation behind Destiny's Child's amazing accomplishments, which included multiplatinum, Grammy-winning R&B singles and albums.

After the history-making girl group dissolved in 2004, Beyoncé carved out for herself a solo career. She thrilled international audiences with spectacular stage shows and took on movie roles, product endorsements, and a signature clothes line. Then at the 2008 Grammys, she enjoyed an inspirational moment when pop legend Tina Turner joined her onstage to deliver a raucous rendition of "Proud Mary." Two months later, Beyoncé married the world's wealthiest rapper and hip-hop entrepreneur, Shawn Corey Carter, aka Jay-Z.

Yet despite—or perhaps as a result of—Beyoncé's meteoric rise to fame and her public transformation from child star to adult phenomenon, she remains an enigma. To fans and casual observers, she is big-hearted and breathtakingly beautiful; to academics and critics alike, she is a study in contrasts—a walking-talking contradiction whose sexy disguises fail to hide a well-ingrained set of conventional values. For starters, her musical proficiency is not something she accidentally acquired while listening to the radio or singing in the church choir. It stems from professional lessons and training—a tight vocal technique with an operatic octave range. Disciplined practice turned innate talent into a finely tuned instrument.

Also, as *the* role model for African American teen girls, her avowal of Christianity, deference for milk (instead of alcohol and tobacco), and gracious southern manners add credibility to a conservative credo. The young performer seems to have avoided the dead ends of drugs, DUIs (driving under the influence) and embarrassing displays of self-abuse and self-indulgence.

But that pristine Beyoncé is not the total Beyoncé. There is another persona the singer calls Sasha—one who bares flesh, bats her eyelashes, and sends out sultry smiles. That sexy, uninhibited alter ego and the jet setter who worships at the feet of the Great God of Commerce are one and the same, and together they tempt Beyoncé to sizzle in bikinis on the cover and inside pages of *Sports Illustrated* and appear in risqué ads for her fashion collection, House of Dereon.

At age 27, Beyoncé, in many ways, has seen it all—chatted with heads of state and industry, hobnobbed with politicians and Hollywood's elite, and traveled the world from hemisphere to hemisphere. But her resumé lacks many of the ordinary rites of passage most upwardly mobile females claim as rightful entitlements: SATs, cheerleading, college mixers, internships, car payments, and first jobs. Gaps exist in Beyoncé's knowledge and emotional development because her promoters reframed and marketed Destiny's Child as an older and more sophisticated act. It was easier and more financially profitable than permitting nature to have free rein. She candidly admits, "My life, my job and responsibilities, and the pressures I've had have forced me to mature faster."[1]

At first, Beyoncé says, her musical compositions were "corny," thus promptly jettisoned by industry insiders as inappropriate. A&R rep (artist and repertoire representative) Theresa LaBarbera Whites and others believed audiences would not relate to juvenile themes of peace, world unity, and such and might consider the group "cheesy" and "bubblegum."[2]

In agreeing to sing and compose more mature music, however, Beyoncé telescoped her adolescence. While wailing of bridges, birthdays, and boyfriends on Destiny's Child's first album, she skipped over many of puberty's most time-intensive tasks and rituals, like sports, specialized teachers for different subjects as in regular high schools, and shifting friendships; other challenges, such as separation from parents and studies abroad, she omitted entirely. Perhaps Beyoncé instinctively knew the clumsiness of trying to emancipate herself from two individuals who headed her business and design team. So she settled instead for buying a Rolls Royce.

Adulthood, of course, not only allowed Beyoncé to feign empowerment and independence, but also gave her unqualified permission to shake her booty, mix sex with sensationalism, and belt out songs like "Survivor" and, later on, "Get Me Bodied." While Sasha (B's alter ego) performed, Beyoncé's inner child—the emotionally inexperienced teen relegated to a corner of her mind—claimed an adolescent's right to experiment, hang out, paint, crack her knuckles, talk on the phone, and binge on fried chicken. (Beyoncé has a lifetime guarantee for free Popeye Chicken.)

Through it all, Beyoncé's postponed adolescence and sexed-up image prompted inconsistent behaviors that barely caused a hiccup in Beyoncé's daily life but disturbed journalists and biographers, who could not quite reconcile the luscious libertine with the demure damsel; the blond-tressed glamour girl with the soft-spoken, well-mannered "church lady" who, according to one reporter, halted a rehearsal mid-song just to bid him farewell.

Writers of all media—electronic, print, or otherwise—continue to follow Beyoncé's every strut and spoken word as if the complete Beyoncé is present, or at least imminent, but despite their perspicacity, she has not yet taken a curtain call. That is because a self-actualized, integrated Beyoncé—an adult who resolves conflicts reasonably and rationally while pursuing her interests, abilities, and talents—has not yet broken through her own image. Like many twenty-somethings, Beyoncé still wanders in the desert of absolutes, not quite ready to emerge into that gray temperate zone in which most people dwell.

Still, that does not mean she lacks authenticity. Look behind the image-boosting brand that she and her public-relations team tout and you glimpse a future Beyoncé. She is much more than the ethnically ambiguous beauty whose talent surpasses her looks and whose looks transcend her entrepreneurial prowess. The young Beyoncé languishes there dressed in jeans and T-shirt. Her face bears hardly a trace of makeup, and in her hand she holds a dish of chocolate ice cream. Maybe she will challenge Jay-Z to a later game of Connect Four (a two-player board game in which players drop discs into a vertically suspended grid until they line up four in a row).[3] Beyoncé is expert at this. Or maybe she and her husband will grab a burger and fries at a Nets game while cheering on the home team. (Beyoncé loves fast food.)

And speaking of youth-oriented pursuits, the future Beyoncé undoubtedly will welcome children into that stately Scarsdale, New York, mansion that she and Jay-Z share. There, Beyoncé can reclaim her country-girl-tomboy roots. With her progeny by her side, she can explore the adolescent pleasures she bypassed as well as pursue more mature interests. These exploits, no doubt, will take advantage of her hard-earned and well-deserved place in the music and entertainment industries.

NOTES

1. Quoted in Kierna Mayo, "Beyoncé Unwrapped," *Teen Hollywood*, August 10, 2003, www.teenhollywood.com (accessed July 14, 2008).

2. Jenny Eliscu, "Beyoncé Knowles of Destiny's Child," *Rolling Stone*, July 6, 2000, www.ebscohost.com (accessed July 7, 2008).

3. Dave Maher, "Beyoncé PWNS Kanye in Connect Four," www.pitchfork-media.com (accessed January 13, 2009).

TIMELINE: EVENTS IN THE LIFE OF BEYONCÉ KNOWLES

1981   Beyoncé Knowles is born on September 4 in Houston, Texas.

1988   Beyoncé's parents sign her up for dance school. Beyoncé wins the first of many beauty pageants and dance contests.

1990   Beyoncé joins Girl's Tyme.

1992   Beyoncé and Girl's Tyme appear on the TV show *Star Search*. The group loses, and Mathew Knowles quits his sales position to become the manager of the group.

1995   The group signs a recording contract with Elektra Records. The girls begin recording an album, but the company drops them several months later.

1996   Columbia Records signs the girls, and they rename themselves Destiny's Child after a Bible verse in the Book of Isaiah.

1997   The single "No, No, No" is released. The song "Killing Time" from the *Men in Black* movie soundtrack also comes out. The girls make in-store appearances in major cities with actor Will Smith.

1998   Destiny's Child's first album is released. "No, No, No" flies up the R&B charts. Destiny's Child records "Get on the Bus" for the movie soundtrack *Why Do Fools Fall in Love?* Whitney Houston invites the group to her birthday party. The group performs with Boyz II Men and other groups.

1999   Destiny's Child releases its second album, *The Writing's on the Wall*. The song "Bills, Bills, Bills" goes to Number 1 on the

U.S. charts in July and hits the Top 10 on the U.K. charts. LaTavia Roberson and LeToya Luckett ask Mathew Knowles not to manage them anymore, whereupon they are fired.

2000   Destiny's Child replaces LeToya Luckett and LaTavia Roberson with Michelle Williams and Farrah Franklin. Farrah leaves the group within a few months. Destiny's Child decides to remain a trio. The threesome goes on tour to market *The Writing's on the Wall*. They open for Christina Aguilera on her megatour. In March the song "Say My Name" hits Number 1 on the charts; "Jumpin' Jumpin'" hits big, too.

2001   Destiny's Child releases the album *Survivor*. In February the group performs before President George W. Bush at the White House. The group teams up with Candie's shoes to launch a vintage shoe line. The group headlines MTV's first TRL ("Total Request Live") during the summer. The girls appear on the cover of *Rolling Stone* and on "Saturday Night Live." After 9/11, Destiny's Child does benefits in NYC and Washington, D.C. The group releases the holiday album *8 Days of Christmas*. Beyoncé takes a solo gig as Carmen in MTV's "Carmen: A Hip-Hopera."

2002   Beyoncé plays Foxxy Cleopatra in the movie *Austin Powers: Goldmember*. Beyoncé signs an endorsement contract with Pepsi-Cola.

2003   Beyoncé appears in *The Fighting Temptations*. She releases her first solo album, *Dangerously in Love*, and the single "Crazy in Love." Beyoncé performs at the Super Bowl XXXVII preshow. She remakes the song "The Closer I Get to You" with Luther Vandross. Beyoncé starts to date Jay-Z after recording "Bonnie & Clyde" on his album, *The Blueprint: The Gift and the Curse*. Beyoncé performs at the Prince's Trust Concert to raise money for disadvantaged children. She also appears at the 46664 concert for AIDS in Cape Town, South Africa. Although objectionable to some people, Beyoncé sings "Crazy in Love" on the steps of Grant's tomb. She appears on the "AFI Life Achievement Award: A Tribute to Robert De-Niro," "The Barbara Walters Special: The 10 Most Fascinating People of 2003," "Punk'd," "V. Graham Norton," "Macy's 4th of July Spectacular," "Boogie," "The Tonight Show with Jay Leno," and "The Oprah Winfrey Show."

2004   Destiny's Child gets together to record its last album, *Destiny Fulfilled*; it is released in November. Beyoncé sings "The Star-Spangled Banner" at Super Bowl XXXVIII. Beyoncé sings with Prince at the Grammy Awards. She tours for a month with Alicia Keys and Missy Elliott, then launches her first perfume, True Star, with Tommy Hilfiger. She appears on "Fade to Black," "Fashion Rocks," "Maxim Hot 100," "Michael Jackson: The One," "The Wayne Brady Show," and "The Oprah Winfrey Show."

2005   Beyoncé and her mother start their clothing line, House of Dereon. Destiny's Child begins its worldwide *Destiny Fulfilled and Lovin' It* tour. Beyoncé stars in the movie *The Pink Panther* with Steve Martin. Destiny's Child performs at the Live 8 Benefit Concert, then announces the group's break-up. She appears on "ESPY Awards," "The Kennedy Center Honors: A Celebration of the Performing Arts," "Rockin' the Corps: An American Thank You," and "The Oprah Winfrey Show."

2006   Beyoncé stars in *Dreamgirls*. She releases her second solo album, *B'Day*. She appears on "Top of the Pops" and "Late Show with David Letterman" and sings the national anthem at the NBA All-Star Game in Houston, Texas. Two PETA (People for the Ethical Treatment of Animals, an animal rights group) members show up at a New York City restaurant and appeal to Beyoncé to stop selling clothes with fur. PETA also writes Beyoncé a letter of concern regarding the treatment of baby alligators in a photo shoot for *B'Day*. The song "Irreplaceable" goes to Number 1 on the charts in the United States.

2007   Beyoncé tours the world with her show *The Beyoncé Experience*. She debuts Diamonds, an Emporio Armani fragrance.

2008   Beyoncé films the movie *Cadillac Records* in which she plays singer Etta James. She sings a duet with Tina Turner at the Grammy Awards. Aretha Franklin gets angry at Beyoncé for referring to Tina Turner as the "Queen" (of Soul). The U.S. Court of Appeals upholds the lower court's decision dismissing the singer Jennifer Armour's copyright infringement suit against Beyoncé. The movie *Obsessed*, in which Beyoncé appears, starts filming.

April   Beyoncé and Jay-Z marry in Scarsdale, New York; a reception is held in Jay-Z's Tribeca penthouse in Manhattan. She starts to record a new album. A wax figure of Beyoncé is unveiled in Los Angeles for a new Tussaud's Wax Museum there.

November   Beyoncé releases her new double album, *I Am . . . Sasha Fierce* to enthusiastic reviews. Two single tracks—"If I Were a Boy" and "Single Ladies (Put a Ring on It)"—climb to the Top 10 by the year's end.

2009   Beyoncé appears at a tribute at the Kennedy Center for the Performing Arts in Washington, D.C., singing the standard, "The Way We Were," for honoree Barbra Streisand. On January 20, Beyoncé performs "At Last" at an inaugural ball for President Barack Obama.

Chapter 1

ROOTS

Seven-year-old Beyoncé Knowles loved family sing-a-longs. She and her mother, Tina Knowles, and her younger sister, Solange, gathered around the piano in their spacious Houston home while Dad tapped out his favorite tunes on the keyboard.

"My parents used to sing to me all the time," Beyoncé wrote. "My dad tells me that as a baby, I would go crazy whenever I heard music, and I tried to dance before I could even walk."[1]

Given these natural inclinations, it was not surprising that when Tina asked first-grader Beyoncé the age-old question, what did you do today in school? Beyoncé shot back that she learned a song. When her mother told her to sing it while she was at the kitchen sink washing dishes, Beyoncé stood up and serenaded her mother. From that time on, she never forgot the exhilaration of performing in front of an audience. It was a pattern Beyoncé adopted at an early age and nurtured through the years while her parents contributed to the process by reinforcing their elder daughter's love of music and appreciating her efforts.

THE NAME GAME

Strong family support guided most decisions in the Knowles household, even before September 4, 1981—the day Beyoncé Giselle Knowles was born at Park Plaza Hospital in Houston, Texas. "My mom claims that it was an easy and relatively painless birth—unlike some of my other entrances," Beyoncé wrote.[2]

Her dad, Mathew, compromised with his wife in naming their first child. Mathew chose the middle name, Giselle; Tina chose their daughter's first name, Beyoncé, to honor her own parents, who lacked for family members to carry on the surname Beyince. Initially Tina's family was dismayed by the name choice. Her father said Beyoncé would later resent the ambiguity of a first name that sounded like a surname, but Tina rebutted the accusation, stating that the name Beyoncé did not necessarily convey a surname to everyone.

Tina may have intuited that her daughter would someday follow in the footsteps of other notable musical artists, such as Prince and Cher, and go by a single name. Beyoncé's unusual name originated from the European lineages of various ancestors. Although her father's African American heritage simplifies one part of the genetic equation, Tina's ethnic inheritance is more complex. Beyoncé's maternal grandmother, Agnez Dereon (born Agnes DeRouen) grew up in Delcambre/New Iberia, Louisiana. Her background resembled a smorgasbord—a mélange of descendants who were Jewish American, African American, Louisiana Creole, and Choctaw Native American. Diversity also dominated the genealogy of Beyoncé's maternal grandfather, Lumas Beyince. Also from Louisiana, he had a mixed ancestry of Chinese, Indonesian, French, and Spanish.

Despite the ethnic bouillabaisse Beyoncé's grandparents contributed, they embraced several similarities. First, all four struggled with poverty as exemplified by Mathew's father, who drove a truck in Gadsden, Alabama, and operated a scrap metal business on the side; Mathew's mother worked days as a maid for a white family, then returned home and knitted quilts for a second income. The Knowles family missed out on the growing prosperity of many Americans in the decades after World War II, when the population exploded mainly because soldiers returned from the war, married, and started families. Mathew's family was so poor that their home lacked indoor plumbing, and they relied on an outhouse. Unlike many baby boomers (those born between 1946 and 1964), Mathew did not grow up in the middle-class comfort typical of many of his white contemporaries.

Racial problems in postwar Alabama—the most racist of the states in the deep South—were intense, with the re-eruption of Ku Klux Klan violence resulting from the twin threats of black voter registration and more liberal economic and educational attitudes toward blacks. Although much of the white population was horrified by Klan-perpetrated murders and mayhem, they also worried about federal intervention into local race relations. Segregationist practices were about to be tested in the nation's political and legal arenas with such federal court decisions as *Brown v.*

Board of Education (the historic 1954 Supreme Court decision to integrate schools) and the Civil Rights Act of 1964, which prohibited discrimination in schools, employment, and public accommodations.

During these turbulent times, the Knowles's modest lifestyle often necessitated that old batteries, refrigerators, and cars be stored in the backyard—a situation that embarrassed Mathew, as it converted his home into a junkyard. Mathew told students at Berklee College of Music in Boston that his parents empathized with their son's discomfort, and when Christmas came, they bought him gifts so he would not feel out of the mainstream.

In a town deeply divided by racist "Jim Crow" laws, Mathew rightfully felt anxious and on the brink of drastic changes. Injustices frequently came up in conversation in the Knowles household. Mathew's mother (a strong woman who attended Lincoln High School in Marion, Alabama, with Coretta Scott King, the wife of Martin Luther King, Jr.) supported desegregation and integration. As a result of Mrs. Knowles's civil rights activism on behalf of her son, Mathew became the first black child to attend Litchfield Junior High and one of the first black students at Gadsden High. Before that he also attended a private Catholic school for blacks and was instructed by white nuns.

MIGHTY OAKS

As a teenager in the 1960s, Mathew joined the ranks of civil rights activists in his home state. He marched in demonstrations in the 1960s and participated in restaurant sit-ins. In high school he was interested in music, but did not aspire to a music career until he attended college, where he shared the dream of discovering and developing musical acts with WFSK (88.1 FM) general manager David Lombard, a student at Vanderbilt University in Nashville (Lombard eventually handled the group En Vogue).

A basketball scholarship made it possible for Mathew to become one of the first African Americans at the University of Tennessee at Chattanooga. During his sophomore year, Mathew met Ronnie Lawson, a coach for Fisk University's Bulldogs basketball team, and Lawson invited Mathew to play for his team. That enticement, together with his own desire to attend a predominantly black college, motivated Mathew to transfer to Fisk University in Nashville, where his mentors included Dr. Winfred David, chair of the business department. Mathew graduated from Fisk in 1974 with degrees in management and economics. Today, he is listed under Fisk's honorary category "Her Sons and Daughters."

TINA KNOWLES

Tina Knowles (nee Celestine Beyince), the youngest of seven children, grew up in a hard-working family in Galveston, Texas. Born January 4, 1954, she attended a Catholic elementary school, and by junior high, belonged to the singing group, the Beltones, modeled after the Supremes and other similar Motown acts. Her father worked the port as a longshoreman, and her mother sewed for her family and for customers. To afford Tina's parochial school costs, her mother tailored clerical garments—robes for the altar boys and cloaks and altar cloths for the priests. "My mother was so talented and so resourceful," Tina said. "People would come to her to make their prom dresses and beautiful formal gowns."[3]

Tina says her mother's Creole traditions influenced her and later Tina's dress designs. Historically, Creole fashions—a blend of European and African styles—were considered radical and politically subversive because of their rejection of certain European elements. Creole dress design strived for a daring, attention-getting appearance, with inventive head wear (turbans and wraps), shorter lengths, and bolder colors (seamstresses often paired bright greens and reds). The vibrancy of color and the unconventionality of design were matched only by the frou-frou-like ornamentation. Agnez sketched dress patterns on paper, cut them out, and then decorated them much like a cake, adding beading, lace, jeweled buttons, and embroidered designs.

Tina applied those same aesthetic standards to designing outfits for the Beltones, and her mother did the actual sewing. Tina says she used as reference points the overall image of The Supremes—how they styled their hair, their costumes, and their manners. Tina did not know it then, but she was actually rehearsing her talents for a later time when she would both design and tailor sequined clothes for a statuesque 5' 7" Beyoncé and other members of Destiny's Child.

THE TINA AND MATHEW SHOW

Tina and Mathew's romantic relationship began in the late 1970s, when Tina, a local Houston bank employee, met Mathew, a sales person for Xerox, at a party. Afterwards, when Mathew wished to contact Tina, he realized he did not know where she worked. One day, a year after they were first introduced, they passed each other on a downtown street. It happened three times the same day, and both Tina and Mathew thought it was an odd coincidence. So Mathew invited the attractive young woman to join him at a restaurant. Tina and Mathew married in 1979, and Beyoncé was born in 1981; her sister, Solange, was born four years later.

WORKING MODELS

From the outset, both of Beyoncé's parents considered their children top priorities. Practical-minded, Tina and Mathew chose traditional careers so they might become strong role models and solid providers. Beyoncé knew about her father's civil rights activism and, after reading in school about the racial struggles of that divisive period, she took great pride in his participation and thought her father showed courage.

A born salesman, Mathew had no shortage of jobs before joining the corporate sector. Between 1975 and 1980, he sold life insurance, telephone equipment, postage meters, and copiers. Eventually he sold high-tech hospital equipment such as CT scanners and MRI machines for Pickering International Medical Supplies. He joined Xerox Corporation around 1979–1980 and established an aggressive marketing record at the company, which earned him Salesman of the Year for the medical division for three consecutive years. The honor came with a six-figure salary, transforming Mathew into a high-paid African American executive, a rarity in the 1980s.

During the late 1980s and 1990s, during Mathew's tenure at Xerox, Houston was home base for many other large companies offering increased opportunities for African American professionals. Houstonians of color with skills and education could apply for a variety of decent-paying positions in a robust job market. At the same time, Tina also set her sights on the so-called fast track. By saving her bank earnings and part-time beautician's salary, she accumulated enough to invest in a hair salon. During the 1980s, the 24-chair Headliners Hair Salon—one of the largest hair styling establishments in Houston—also became one of the most profitable. "We catered to the professional woman so we had judges and attorneys," Tina said.[4]

Entrepreneurs like Tina found the business climate for blacks slowly improving thanks to Houston's Minority, Women, Disadvantaged, and Small Business Enterprise Program (MWDBE/SBE), which allowed women and minorities to compete equally for city contracts. Project categories included professional services (e.g., architecture, accounting, computer programming) and purchasing services (goods and nonprofessional services such as printing and security). In 1984, only $2.5 million in construction, purchasing, and professional service contracts went to minorities and women. By 1993, $83 million was distributed.[5]

BLACK POWER

Despite progress in race relations during the 1990s, racism existed during this period in Houston and still exists today to some extent, as in most large urban areas in the United States. But groups like the Greater Houston Partnership—an organization responsible for stimulating economic growth—challenged old attitudes and prejudices, and local discrimination battles were partly resolved through a 1979 landmark environmental case: *Bean v. Southwestern Waste Management, Inc.* In this case homeowners used the Civil Rights Act of 1968 to try to prevent the establishment of a waste facility in a predominantly black neighborhood in Houston. Before that, more than 80 percent of Houston's garbage landfills and incinerators were in largely black neighborhoods.[6] Similar litigation took place in other parts of the country, and activists organized the National People of Color Environmental Leadership Summit in Washington, D.C., which protested the lack of environmental protection in areas in which black, poor, and working-class people lived.

By 1981, the year Beyoncé was born, Houston had evolved into a more progressive place to raise a family. Tina and Mathew moved into a large six-bedroom home in an integrated, upper middle-class section of the Third Ward. Beyoncé says she lived in a house as nicely situated and as large as the one in which she lives now.

In 1992, the cost of living in Houston was relatively low, with the average price for a new home costing $92,736.[7] Houston's public school system, with nearly 195,000 students in 1994, was one of the nation's largest, but its funding was low, barely $3,424 per student. (Nationally, the average per-pupil funding was $6,084, with a low of $3,203 in Utah and a high of $9,429 in New Jersey.[8]) Around 1990, however, the Houston Independent School District began instituting reform measures. The school board drafted a mission statement favoring decentralization and focusing on performance goals. In 1994, when the district hired Rod Paige, its first African American superintendent, an accountability system went into effect, as well as a peer review program that included performance contracts for administrators and incentive pay for teachers. By 1997, the school system, with its predominantly minority enrollment, had substantially improved in student and teacher performance and management.

HOUSTON'S RECORDING STUDIOS

Houston's public school system was lacking in many respects, but its cultural scene was thriving. The city had a long history of record labels, studios and record-manufacturing plants going back to the 1950s and

1960s. Among these venues were Steffek Records, Tantara Records (co-owned by band manager Richard Ames and his brother Steve), ACA Studios, Doyle Jones Recording Studio, and Mickey Gilley's Jones Recording Studio. By 2000, more than 150 studios operated in the Houston and East Texas areas.

One of the most prominent studios was Gold Star, founded originally as a venue for country music artists by record producer Bill Quinn. In the late 1940s, blues singers recorded there and enjoyed commercial success, and when the 1950s came along, the studio welcomed rock 'n roll stars such as the "Big Bopper" Richardson, who recorded "Chantilly Lace," and Johnny Preston, of "Running Bear" fame. In 1971 Gold Star Studio changed ownership and was renamed Sugar Hill Studio, hosting such musical greats as Janis Joplin, Sunny and the Sunliners, Ricky Nelson, and Freddy Fender. By 1986, many Tejano recording artists patronized Sugar Hill; a decade later, so did Destiny's Child and Beyoncé. The oldest continuously operating studio in Texas and the Southwest, Sugar Hill celebrated its 65th anniversary in October 2006, and is now co-owned by the famous record producer Dan Workman.

SUBURBIA IN THE 1990s

In Harris County, Texas, where the Knowles lived in 1990, people believed that education opened the proverbial doors to upward mobility. Twenty-five percent of the adult population had a bachelor's degree or higher, according to the U.S. Census Bureau.[9]

In school if Beyoncé had studied the demographics of her community, she would have discovered that 66 percent of the Harris County population was native Texan—like herself.[10] The median household income was $30,970, and only 12.5 percent of families were below the poverty level.[11] In 1993, Houston was ethnically divided—about 28 percent of the city's 1.6 million population was African American; 28 percent was Hispanic, and the remainder was white.[12]

COMFORTABLE LIFESTYLE

The combined incomes of the Knowles family guaranteed that Beyoncé and her sister would enjoy privileged childhoods. Nine-year-old Beyoncé described her family's Christmas in 1990 as a traditional Norman-Rockwell-like holiday. On Christmas Eve her family sang carols, decorated the tree, and danced. Usually they attended midnight Mass at St. Mary's Catholic Church, after which Tina and Mathew exchanged gifts.

In the morning, while Tina was still in bed, Beyoncé and Solange ran downstairs and counted up their presents, gathering them in piles so they could more quickly tear off the wrappings later on and enjoy their gifts. Foreshadowing their adult lives, Beyoncé and Solange entertained their parents with a musical performance.

In the weeks before Christmas, the Knowles family decorated the exterior of their house with lights; the interior sparkled with garlands and stockings. A tree adorned with white lights and mauve and green trimmings stood in a corner of the room. Each year the family added one special glass or ceramic ornament to the tree. On Christmas Day, friends and relatives dropped by throughout the day, and the family later sat down to a traditional dinner: turkey, ham, dressing, dirty rice, candied yams, green beans, sweet potato pie, wine, and eggnog with brandy.

SCHOOL DAZE

Because of Houston's low-rated school system, affluent families in the 1980s favored private schools. Beyoncé attended two Catholic elementary schools—Saint James and St. Mary's Montessori School. With class sizes of 10 to 15 children, the school could offer Beyoncé more individual attention than she would have in a public school.

Teachers positively reinforced Beyoncé's study and academic skills, but schoolmates sometimes teased her and said nasty things. This eroded her self-image, but never more so than one morning when Beyoncé, a fourth-grader at the time, awakened to look in the mirror and see a growth on her lip. Horrified, she attempted to scrape it off, but to her dismay, the dark blemish remained, even when she applied lipstick. Naturally, the boys in her class and in the schoolyard ridiculed her, ostracizing her with their claim that she had the "cooties."[13]

Insecurities about her body also plagued her. "When I was little, my head was smaller and I looked like I had big Dumbo ears," she said.[14] She also was taunted about her weight, other kids using words like "chunky" or "chubby." Then there was the reality of her unusual moniker. She says it became another reason for children to tease her, and during morning roll calls, she felt like hiding under her desk. She says she disliked drawing attention to herself in any way, so she hardly spoke in class, never raised her hand, and pretty much pretended she was invisible.

One reason for this behavior was that certain boys liked Beyoncé, and she did not know what to say to them. Her silence backfired, however, as some classmates thought her a snob. This would not be the first time people misjudged her.

Beyoncé says her quiet demeanor always earned her an "Excellent" in conduct, but she never felt she fit in with her classmates. Maybe it was because Beyoncé never exchanged confidences with students while in class. She feared a rebuke from the teacher, and if, for example, she was called on to go to the blackboard and solve a math problem, she became extremely nervous even though she was a good student who received mainly As and Bs. Despite decent grades, however, academics did not come easily to Beyoncé, and she had to study hard. She loved math, but often struggled with it, and long division was especially challenging. When a boy in her class called her "dumb," she believed it.[15] Beyoncé always cared too much about other people's opinions of her and her self-esteem was damaged by this preoccupation.

To boost her confidence, her parents hired a tutor when she was in seventh grade. Miss Little, an older woman and Beyoncé's second-grade teacher, was strict, and Beyoncé was scared of her and her long nails, glasses, habit of peeling apples, and scary-sounding voice. She begged her mother not to send her for tutoring, but her parents' decision prevailed. Later, Beyoncé revised her opinion of Miss Little and remembered her and the experience positively.

DANCE LESSONS

Another self-esteem tool was the dance lessons that Mathew and Tina enrolled Beyoncé in because they felt they would improve her posture and help her make more friends. Beyoncé's teacher—Darlette Johnson—was the first person to persuade Beyoncé that she had musical talent, contributing greatly to Beyoncé's career by instilling a sense of confidence in the youngster as well as discipline and a positive attitude.

On an "Ellen" Degeneres show that aired around Beyoncé's 25th birthday, Johnson told her former pupil how she first recognized Beyoncé's extraordinary vocal abilities: Beyoncé was the last child to be picked up after dance lessons that day. While waiting for the youngster's parents, Johnson started singing and Beyoncé finished the song. As Beyoncé hit a high note, Johnson said, "Sing it again," and as soon as Beyoncé's parents arrived, Johnson cried out, "She can sing! She really can sing."[16]

IMAGINE HER A STAR

Miss Johnson showed her faith in the seven-year-old's singing abilities by urging Beyoncé to enter an upcoming school talent show—even though Beyoncé became frightened before school performances. "She would literally have tears in her eyes," Johnson recalled. "I would have to hold on to her and tell her, it's okay, take deep breaths." After the panic attack passed, however, a transformation took place. The youngster would go onstage and "sing like a woman."[17] This is exactly what happened at St. Mary's talent show in 1988.

The contest was in the auditorium, and both Beyoncé's parents came to watch. When she peeked out from backstage, she saw a crowd of teachers, classmates, and parents seated on yellow plastic chairs. The room was hot and everyone tried to cool themselves with hastily improvised paper fans.

Beyoncé was so shaken with fear that Johnson had to chide her to hustle onstage. Beyoncé still remembers walking out and feeling disconnected, as if she could not speak, much less sing. She stood rigid, almost catatonic, in front of a sea of strange faces and did not know what to do. But when the familiar music started, she calmed down and became another person entirely—stronger, more poised, and eager to share her vocal talents. Beyoncé the Entertainer materialized as she sang the now classic John Lennon composition, "Imagine."

Mathew said he knew his daughter was musically gifted the moment she sang the first few measures of the haunting Beatles tune. Tina could not believe this was the same introverted little girl who had difficulty making new friends. In front of her now was a young woman, her lips parted, her arms spread wide as she uttered the gently affirming lyrics.

Amazed at their daughter's prodigious talent—Beyoncé's parents had never heard her rehearse the piece—Mathew and Tina regarded each other with confusion. Beyoncé remembers the smiles on her parents' faces and how she felt surprised at her own delivery. "I'm not even sure where I found the courage," she said. "All I know is that I felt at home on that stage, more so than anywhere else."[18]

It was a home she would cherish more and more as her star rose higher and brighter.

NOTES

1. Beyoncé Knowles, Kelly Rowland, and Michelle Williams, *Soul Survivors: The Official Autobiography of Destiny's Child* (New York: Regan Books/HarperCollins, 2002), 9.

2. Ibid.

3. Quoted in Warner Roberts, "Tina Knowles: Pop Star's Mom Sews Some Diva-licious Threads," September 2007, www.htexas.com (accessed April 15, 2008).

4. Quoted by TOURE, "Cover Story: A Woman Possessed," *Rolling Stone*, March 4, 2004, www.find.galegroup.com (accessed April 15, 2008).

5. City of Houston, Affirmative Action and Contract Compliance, "Minority, Women, Disadvantaged, and Small Business Enterprise Program (MWDBE/SBE)," revised August 14, 2006.

6. Robert D. Bullard, "Environmental Justice For All," *The New Crisis*, Jan. 1, 2003, 24–26.

7. www.pbs.org/newshour/backgrounders/school_funding.html (accessed May 8, 2008).

8. Ibid.

9. U.S. Census Bureau, "Social Characteristics: 1990. Harris County, Texas," www.factfinder.census.gov (accessed April 16, 2008).

10. Ibid.

11. U.S. Census Bureau, "USA Counties 1994, Harris, TX, General Profile," www.factfinder.census.gov (accessed April 16, 2008).

12. Ibid.

13. Quoted by Jodi Lynn Bryson, "Ooh, Child: Destiny Talks," *Teen Magazine*, August 2001, www.search.ebscohost.com (accessed April 16, 2008).

14. Quoted by Jangee Dunn, "A Date with Destiny," *Rolling Stone*, May 24, 2001. www.ebscohost.com (accessed April 16, 2008).

15. Beyoncé et al., 11.

16. Ibid.

17. Quoted by Mimi Valdes, "The Metamorphosis," *Vibe*, July 25, 2003, www.bookrags.com (accessed April 16, 2008).

18. Ibid.

Chapter 2

BOOT CAMP

The moment seven-year-old Beyoncé intoned the first notes of John Lennon's peace ballad, "Imagine," and surrendered to the moving lyrics and plaintive melody, she recognized her bliss. Before that, Beyoncé speculated on becoming a hair stylist like her mother or perhaps a psychologist. "I really like talking to people and finding out why they do what they do," Beyoncé said.[1]

After that one performance, however, she realized her passion would always be music and the creativity and vocal nuances she could bring to it. "I was like, Oh Lord, this is amazing," Beyoncé said. "So I knew I wanted to be a singer."[2] From then on, Beyoncé begged to enter talent shows and other competitions—she won first place every time.

Some shows were "glorified beauty pageants," Beyoncé wrote,[3] but she always enjoyed the talent portion The beauty portion was boring to her, as she was a tomboy who did not like to fuss over clothes, avoided wearing dresses or carrying purses, and often went barefoot.

BEAUTY PAGEANTS

One of the earliest contests she entered was sponsored by the People's Workshop for the Visual and Performing Arts, a nonprofit organization that showcased local talent. Beyoncé sang in the Baby Junior category (children under age seven) and won the 1989 Sammy Award for female pop vocalist. A video of this performance shows her in a blue-sequined dress similar to the character Dorothy's costume in *The Wizard of Oz*. Shuffling from side to side with her eyes focused on the stars, Beyoncé sang "Home" from the Broadway musical *The Wiz*. Even at that early age, her showmanship set off sparks. Accepting her award, Beyoncé said, "I would like to thank the judges for picking me, my parents, who I love—I love you, Houston." After that, she blew a big kiss. In hindsight Beyoncé called herself a "huge ham who got carried away with show biz and wanted to strut my stuff."[4]

Just because Beyoncé was passionate about music did not mean she turned in flawless performances. To help her improve, Beyoncé's parents critiqued her performances, giving her feedback on her vocals and dance moves. As a result of this advice, she improved. "I had so many trophies I could barely walk from my bed to the door," Beyoncé wrote.[5] But the youngster reveled in more than prizes. She enjoyed creating dance routines and arranging vocals. To Beyoncé, everything connected with music was fun.

SONG-AND-DANCE ACTS

Beyoncé generated enthusiasm each time she appeared onstage. Eventually she caught the attention of a Houston woman interested in assembling a singing group. She invited Beyoncé to audition. Shortly after joining Girl's Tyme, Beyoncé became lead singer for the group. The second- and third-grade members fluctuated in number between six or seven girls at any one time.

Some months later Andretta Tillman, a friend of one of the group's founders, invested money in the troupe and became manager. Besides rehearsing, the girls watched videos of the Jackson 5, the Supremes, and En Vogue, a successful girl group of the day, in order to imitate their style and dance steps. Although each En Vogue member had her personal look, together they produced great harmonies and routines.

"We didn't have time for boys," Kelly Rowland said. "We just wanted to rehearse."[6] In 1990, they appeared at local gigs like the Miss Black Houston Metroplex Pageant, AstroWorld, and high school concerts. All the while, Girl's Tyme, which renamed itself Something Fresh, canvassed the area for new talent. Then Beyoncé suggested that her close friend, LeToya Luckett, might add to the pool of talent. She would be an asset to the group because Beyoncé and she had starred together in the school play *Pinocchio*. So LeToya auditioned and joined Girl's Tyme in 1991. By then, Kelly lived with the Knowles family because her mother worked as a nanny in another state. Mathew and Tina thought that if Kelly moved in with them, they could avoid her and her mother's long-distance commutes for rehearsals. Despite conflicting media reports, however, Tina maintained that she and Mathew never officially adopted Kelly or applied for legal guardianship.[7]

By 1992, the six-person group added producer-songwriter Alonzo Jackson to its list of promoters. Everyone believed the timing was perfect for a girl group to hit big. At the 1992 Sammy Davis Jr. Awards at Houston's Wortham Center, the girls sang about boys and world unity, combining R&B, rap, and pop and a lot of fast-moving, foot-stomping choreography. Beyoncé even coaxed an embarrassed boy onstage and beguiled him with romantic lyrics. Beyoncé's growing confidence came from her pursuit of three career goals that she listed in a video of herself at age 11: a gold album, a platinum follow-up album, and writer-producer credits on another album. (She attained these goals by the time she was 20.)[8]

Determined to snare a record contract, the girls tried various strategies, including experimenting with a series of catchy group names: Something Fresh, Borderline, Cliché, The Dolls, and Self Expression. In late 1997, Beyoncé's mom dubbed the group "Destiny" while scanning the Bible for ideas. The addition of "Child" resulted from the need to differentiate the group from other "Destiny" groups, so Mathew tacked on "Child," as he felt it implied a rebirth.

PRACTICE MAKES PERFECT

Beyoncé started regular vocal practices at age seven, when she began singing in the church choir. She also took voice and dance lessons and the group practiced all day long in the summers. During the school week the girls might start rehearsing around 2 p.m. on Saturday and not finish until midnight.[9] Sometimes the girls practiced in the Knowles living room, where their high-spirited dance moves broke, at various times, a table, a glass panel from a cabinet, and various artworks.

Another convenient practice venue was Headliners Hair Salon, which Tina owned and managed. The customers were a captive audience of mainly black women whom Beyoncé got to know and respect. Sometimes and especially when the women were seated under hair dryers, Girl's Tyme performed for them. If the critical feedback was positive, the girls collected tips or Tina treated them to a trip to AstroWorld, an amusement park similar to Six Flags. But the girls limited the fun and games after they were warned that dedication, commitment, and hard work were necessary for *any* degree of success. Still, they did not yet know to what extent a pop music career curtailed normal activities. When they saw videos of other groups, they did not truly comprehend the exhaustive preparations that went into video production.

When in 1992 Beyoncé's dad began to co-manage Girl's Tyme with Andretta Tillman (until her death from lupus in 1997), he increased the number and intensity of practices. His stiff protocol became known as Knowles Boot Camp. It did not help that Beyoncé was a perfectionist who "always wanted to be like Janet Jackson or Michael Jackson—those types of people," said Vernell Jackson, a friend of the Knowles family.[10]

During summer mornings the girls sang as they jogged in Houston's Memorial Park—a strategy Mathew used to increase their endurance. Everyone disliked the lengthy runs but conceded they served as an antidote to early-day sleepiness or confusion. The girls learned to appreciate "the great outdoors" while they exercised and toned their bodies. During this time, Mathew not only built a stagelike wooden rehearsal deck in the Knowles backyard, but also hired a professional model to show the girls how to walk properly in heels. He also coached them on how to ad lib between songs and answer interview questions from reporters and other media people.

Then, too, a healthy diet was part of the Knowles success formula. It was recommended that Beyoncé lose weight, so she ate Lean Cuisine frozen meals or consumed skinless chicken breasts, turkey, fruit, vegetables, soup, and/or crackers. She cut back drastically on pizza, ice cream, soda, and sweets. This often engendered resentment over her inability to eat like a "normal" teen. Meanwhile Solange, Beyoncé's little sister, practiced, too. At age two, she joined a children's dance troupe, and she and Beyoncé regularly begged their mother's friends to watch and comment on their performances.

For this and other reasons, by 2001, Tina was typed by many in the media as a stage mother. Her chaperone and fashion duties with Destiny's Child and later her close physical proximity to Beyoncé during tours and project negotiations contributed to the rumor, but she denied encouraging either of her daughters to go into entertainment because she and Mathew never wanted to live vicariously through Beyoncé and Solange.[11]

SECRET SINGERS

Patrons of Tina's Headliners Hair Salon knew about Beyoncé's practice sessions, but her school friends did not. Beyoncé believed that if she told people, they would think she was a snob or tease her about record deals and pretensions to fame. Her classmates never figured out why she did not hang out with them on weekends. She and Kelly were just considered the "mysteries of middle school."[12] Another reason Beyoncé and Kelly withheld information was that they were cautioned about involvements with boys. For a long time, Kelly's boyfriend and Lindell, Beyoncé's steady date, did not know the girls sang with a group.

In 2000, when Michelle Williams joined Destiny's Child, Michelle confided that she also kept her talent secret—even when a college professor suggested she join a vocal group and not waste her ability. Then one day a musician-friend told her he played with R&B singer Monica's band. Michelle joked that if Monica ever needed another vocalist, she could call on Michelle. To her amazement, Michelle got that opportunity and left college to pursue it. Michelle believed if you were meant to make music your career, life would lead you in that direction.

MAJORING IN MUSIC

School gave Beyoncé further opportunities to hone her musical skills. At the Houston magnet school, Parker Music Academy, where Beyoncé studied piano and chorus two to three days a week, each of the eight to ten students in Beyoncé's fourth-grade class had his or her own piano and headset. Beyoncé also took traditional classes in reading, arithmetic, physical education, and other required subjects. During Beyoncé's year at Parker, the 800 children enrolled there performed in nursing homes and other venues such as Houston's Galleria. Twice a year, at the holiday season and the end of the school year, students gave recitals. (In 2002, Parker Elementary was selected as the National Grammy Signature Elementary School by the Grammy Foundation.)

Professional musician Theola Booker, who instructed Beyoncé in piano at Parker, remembered her as an attractive, cooperative, and focused child, especially when engaged in an activity of special interest to her. "While everyone else was practicing scales and chords, she would be wandering off into composition and making up her own songs,"[13] Booker said. Beyoncé's parents provided emotional support for their daughter, and to this day, Beyoncé and her parents contribute financially to music education in Texas public schools. In 2004, Beyoncé was named one of three honorary chairs of the Texas Music Project, which provides grant money to schools.

AFTER SCHOOL HOURS

Beyoncé attributes much of her success to her parents' support of music. Tina and Mathew allowed the girls to rehearse on weekends and to attend various performances. They also put up with the girls' constant focus on achieving stardom. "I think we were the most hungry girls I've ever met," Beyoncé said in 2000.[14] The girls became so driven that they did not want to play, go outside, or do anything unless it related to music videos or performances. "It was our whole life," Beyoncé said. "We weren't happy unless we were onstage."[15] The Knowles home was a perfect environment for this all-consuming passion. Solange had recently come on board at age four, when she delivered her first public performance at a local amusement park, singing Sharice's "I Love Your Smile." Solange did not know it then, but one day she would open for Destiny's Child.

FRIENDS AND FUN

Although Beyoncé practiced as much as eight hours a day, she still enjoyed some normal activity in her life. With Kelly as bunkmate, sleep at the Knowles house was a pajama party every night. Tina screamed for them to quiet down; otherwise the two girls would talk and laugh all night in their shared room that they decorated together. "Mickey Mouse" was the design theme: lamps, sheets, alarm clock. One night Beyoncé and Kelly decided to draw mouse ears on the walls and carpet with a magic marker, but Beyoncé's mom put a fast stop to that. The girls also let off some steam between practices. They used a sheet to make a hammock that they attached to the staircase railing. Sometimes they also took mattresses from the bedrooms and slid them down the stairs. Once in a while Beyoncé went to a birthday party or slumber party, and church attendance also gave her an opportunity to interact with kids her own age.

Tina made sure her daughter's life was a healthy balance of work and play. Still, Beyoncé's basic social network was restricted to the members of her singing group. If she missed out on activities because of rehearsals or performances, they usually were extracurricular activities such as cheerleading and sports, and casual friendships also were denied, as they usually resulted from serendipitous encounters at libraries, community centers, and parks. On the other hand, Tina and Mathew encouraged Beyoncé to use her creative energies to enjoy herself by writing songs and poems, making clothes, and inventing dance steps.

As a result, Beyoncé had mixed feelings regarding the constant togetherness of her girl group. She loved the companionship of dressing, eating, and singing together, but she did have reservations about sharing her room and parents with other persons besides Solange. In the beginning Beyoncé had a difficult time sharing the phone, her closet, and her clothes with Kelly. The two girls also had very different styles: Kelly preferred to sleep with the music on and was very neat. Beyoncé liked quiet while sleeping and was inclined to keep a messy room.

STAR SEARCH

Unlike many kids who crave instant gratification, Beyoncé and her singing partners focused on the long-range goals of the music industry—record contracts, cross-country tours, and name recognition. They felt their hard work had paid off in 1992 when they landed a slot on *Star Search*, a talent television show hosted by Ed McMahon. The show gave wannabes a chance to perform before a national audience. Ten thousand people auditioned for the show each year—either in person or on tape; only about 250 actually qualified for the show. The winners of weekly shows competed for a grand prize.

The day of the competition finally came and the six members of Girl's Tyme raced onto the stage wearing jean shorts with purple, lime, and white-colored satin jackets. Although they were well rehearsed and well prepared, the group later said that nothing went as expected. The girls chose a rap-type song rather than a song that showcased their harmonies, and the biggest upset was that producers placed them in a category in which they competed with 30-year-olds in a rock band. When the judges awarded the group three stars, Girl's Tyme knew it was all over. Tears ran down their cheeks as they fled off stage. Beyoncé and her colleagues tried to act like professionals, but the disappointment overwhelmed them. "We thought our lives were over," Beyoncé wrote. "That was my first time I lost something that I really wanted to win."[16]

PICK YOURSELF UP, DUST YOURSELF OFF

The next day Mathew chaperoned everyone to Disneyland (the show was taped in Orlando, Florida), and Beyoncé and the other girls stopped crying long enough to go on the rides. By day's end, they were almost happy, but when the show aired, Beyoncé and the other girls grieved again, despite Tina's surprise gumbo party. "We cried ourselves to sleep that night," Beyoncé wrote. "My Mickey Mouse pillow was drenched."[17]

After the *Star Search* debacle, the girls thought hard about disbanding. But Mathew provided some objectivity to the girls' emotionalism. True, they had delivered a lousy performance, but it was only one TV show. Did they think that one show should determine their entire future? Mathew also reminded them they had invested a lot of hard work and love in this field. The girls gradually realized that the loss was a learning experience because in real life, no one wins everything. After considering these points, Beyoncé and the other girls agreed to stay together. "The meeting was adjourned," Beyoncé wrote, "with a pillow fight."[18]

NOTES

1. Quoted in Jeannine Amber, "A Fashionable Life," *Essence,* September 2006, www.find.galegroup.com (accessed April 27, 2008).

2. Quoted by Toure, "A Woman Possessed," *Rolling Stone,* March 4, 2004, www.find.galegroup.com (accessed April 27, 2008).

3. Quoted in Beyoncé Knowles, Kelly Rowland, and Michelle Williams, *Soul Survivors: The Official Autobiography of Destiny's Child* (New York: Regan/HarperCollins, 2002), 15.

4. Quoted in Knowles et al., 16.

5. Ibid.

6. Quoted in Adrian Thrills, "Kelly Rowland Steps Out of the Shadow of Beyoncé," *Herald Sun,* January 7, 2008, www.news.com.au/heraldsun (accessed April 27, 2008).

7. Lynn Norment, "The Untold Story of How Tina and Mathew Knowles Created the Destiny's Child Gold Mine—Interview," *Ebony,* September 2001, www.findarticles.com (accessed April 15, 2008).

8. "Beyoncé Knowles," www.lyricsstudio.com (accessed September 4, 2008).

9. Knowles et al., 58.

10. Ibid.

11. Norment.

12. Quoted in Knowles et al., 64.

13. Quoted in telephone interview with Theola Booker, March 4, 2008.

14. Knowles et al., 65.

15. Quoted in Richard Harrington, "Spotlight—Destiny's Child's Growing Pains," *Washington Post,* September 15, 2000, N17.

16. Quoted by Billy Johnson, Jr.

17. Quoted in Knowles et al., 71.

18. Quoted in Knowles et al., 72.

Chapter 3

MAKING MUSIC

Although Girl's Tyme lost on *Star Search* in 1992, Beyoncé and her preteen partners knew that this was not the only way to score a record contract. There were other strategies such as appearing on a showcase (a public event that gives local talent an opportunity to perform), but first they would have to polish their vocal and dance skills. In the months after *Star Search*, the girls reviewed their performance tape and could now see their mistakes more easily. We "messed up," they agreed.[1]

So they devised a new plan. They would (a) get fit and trim, (b) rehearse every day, (c) compose new songs, (d) learn to sing a cappella, (e) create new routines, (f) endure despite the frustration, (g) quit watching *Star Search,* and (h) listen to Motown tapes and recordings of Anita Baker and Donny Hathaway. Mathew added two additional goals: Girl's Tyme would perform at one local venue per week during the school year and two venues per week during summer (e.g., Houston rodeos and the Third Ward's Southwestern Bell African-American Arts Festival). The girls also traveled to San Francisco to record so-called demo tapes to mail to record executives.

Mathew also decided to review his contributions and, as a result, he quit his sales position with Xerox so he could concentrate full-time on molding Girl's Tyme into the best girl group in the country. Tina objected, however, despite knowing her husband was smart, as she also knew he was a risk taker. "When he believes in something or someone, the building can fall, but he will never give up," she said.[2] Mathew's unilateral decision to leave his corporate position soon had positive—as well as negative— repercussions for the Knowles family.

MATHEW AND MOTOWN

To function as a dynamic team player for Girl's Tyme, Mathew reinvented himself. No longer would he play the role of sales wunderkind employed by a large prestigious company. He now assumed the role of a determined dad with faith in his daughter's talents. He lacked an exact game plan, but Mathew drew on memories of successful people in the music industry. For many years he had revered and respected Berry Gordy, the founder of Motown Records. So for lack of a better strategy, Mathew emulated Gordy, modeling himself after the man who developed the sound of 1950s and 1960s vocal groups such as the Drifters and the Supremes. Since Mathew knew Gordy performed everything in-house, including commissioning the services of choreographers, stylists, producers, and writers, as well as teaching his artists etiquette and how to project glamour, Mathew would do likewise. Since Gordy felt these attributes were fundamental to the music industry, Mathew would take the identical approach.

At the same time that Mathew integrated Gordy's vision into his, he began to quarrel with Tina. Differing perspectives and stubbornness divided the couple. Tina was convinced Mathew's plan was unrealistic, especially because they were currently confronted by tax problems. To make enough money, Tina worked 16-hour days, but then Mathew would spend thousands of dollars on a photo shoot. "I felt the group was more important to him than his family," Tina said.[3] Tina finally sold their house for below-market price value and relocated to an apartment with Solange, Beyoncé, and Kelly. Meanwhile Mathew took a course in artist management at Houston Community College and spent the next six months away from the family.

While Tina became depressed, Beyoncé repressed memories of that time. At age 12, she knew that solutions for marital discord might eventually result in separation and divorce, but "it was such a painful time that I erased a lot of those memories from my head," Beyoncé wrote.[4]

SAY A LITTLE PRAYER

Beyoncé turned to the church for support. While Tina prayed for her marriage, Beyoncé begged for success. Success meant a record contract and a music career, but Beyoncé believed it also was connected to her parents' future happiness. The congregation of St. John's United Methodist Church also prayed on behalf of the girls. The family felt validated by the congregation's efforts, which inspired the girls to try harder.

Beyoncé's religious fervor went beyond simple devotion. On some level, she knew her faith would help her manage and cope with her parents' six-month separation, as well as the ups and downs of the entertainment industry. "God has a plan," Beyoncé said, "and God is in control of everything."[5] An active congregant since she was a child, Beyoncé faced her problems with calmness and serenity. The church was the safe harbor where she felt she could be honest and true to herself. "Every time I go to church, I feel like I'm baptized," she said.[6] The church rejuvenated Beyoncé and gave her perspective and a positive outlook, and she felt it would prevent mistakes from overwhelming her so she could start over again.

Even during the tumultuous period when LaTavia and LeToya left Destiny's Child, Beyoncé consoled herself with the thought that God watched over her and weeded out people on the periphery of her life. Sometimes she attributed mysterious happenings to God's power, not knowing how else to explain them. Her partners felt similarly and each was bound to Destiny's Child as much by belief in God as by friendship. Before going onstage, the girls always said a prayer: "God bless our voices, let our melodies be tight. Let our dances be tight. God, we ask you to fill us up with your light. We have no reason to be sad or negative. Thank you, God, for bringing us to each other."[7]

THE TWO BEYONCÉS

Offstage Beyoncé shared a prayer with her colleagues, but onstage Beyoncé shared the glory with Sasha, her alter ego. As a child, Beyoncé acted quiet and shy in school and when Girl's Tyme started to perform regularly, she became even more shut-mouthed. She said nothing to her peers about her R&B gigs, and no one, of course, knew of her more assertive and less inhibited counterpart: the wild and crazy Sasha.

At Welch Middle School, Beyoncé slipped back into a submissive role. She became a polite, hard-working, but private student. This demeanor became even more exaggerated when her first cousin, Angie Beyince, warned Beyoncé that girl students might cut off Beyoncé's long hair as a rite of initiation. Beyoncé already was frightened at the prospect of starting a new school, but the threat of losing her hair nearly panicked her. For the first six months at Welch Middle School, Beyoncé wore her hair in a bun, fearful of what might happen. She also kept her "double life" to herself, for she believed the students might consider her an ego-driven brat or pressure her with unrealistic expectations. But when the school day ended, she was more like a typical teenager. She rollerskated, talked on the phone, and enjoyed joking and exchanging confidences with friends.

THE FAB FOUR

After Welch Middle School, Beyoncé attended the High School for the Performing and Visual Arts with its approximately 700 students, but she also remained with Girl's Tyme. Despite several girls' comings and goings, everyone in the group remained friends. Around 1991–1992, Ashley Davis (who went on to perform with Prince as Tamar Davis), joined Girl's Tyme, but later quit the group. After Davis's exit, Mathew helped Kelly and Beyoncé draft two more singer-dancers: LeToya and LaTavia.

Beyoncé also attended Alief Elsik High School for several months in ninth grade, and during this time she finally switched from dressing like a tomboy in jeans, baby T-shirts, and platform tennis shoes to making a fashion statement. Like her mother, Beyoncé began shopping in vintage stores and favored classic suits with pencil-thin skirts and tailored jackets, which she considered mature and wore every day.

Fashion went by the wayside, however, when home schooling/tutoring replaced high school and a conventional education after recording Destiny's Child's first album and scheduling studio time became a priority. It also put an end to fun lunches, breaks between classes, and friendly gab sessions in the hallways. Compared to public school with its more laid-back, people-oriented fringe benefits, LeToya called the group's tutoring schedule "high impact."[8]

Kelly and Beyoncé also continued taking voice lessons, which they had begun at age eight, from David Brewer, a vocal coach and international opera tenor associated with the Houston Ebony Opera (Brewer is currently based in Berlin, Germany). In later conversations with the media, Brewer claimed he "developed and guided"[9] the careers of Beyoncé, Kelly, and LeToya since the three were children. In 2000, Brewer claimed that he, instead of Mathew, contributed more to the success of Destiny's Child.[10]

Later, Mathew deflected Brewer's accusation that the former took credit for Beyoncé's success. In the mid 1990s, however, success seemed elusive, and Beyoncé felt pressured by it. She thought if the group failed, she would be blamed and she agonized over this until she came up at last with a logical rationale that alleviated her anxieties: She reasoned that her mother owned a profitable hair salon and her father was an educated, degreed, and competent man capable of holding a variety of positions. Also, she knew her parents had not sacrificed their lifestyle out of a fear of poverty. Although Mathew and Tina were separated for six months, reconciling later in 1993 when Mathew was no longer a corporate executive, the family still enjoyed middle-class amenities. Beyoncé decided her parents would achieve their goals independent of Girl's Tyme's success. If the group failed, her parents would regroup and prosper anyway, so she relaxed and eased the pressure off herself.

No sooner did Beyoncé reconcile those issues then Girl's Tyme appeared at the Black Expo Juneteenth Festival and producer Daryl Simmons from Silent Partner Productions/Elektra offered the group a contract. At long last and after dozens of demo tapes, bios, and photos had been mailed to record executives, a company had faith in Girl's Tyme. Coincidentally, Mathew followed up with Teresa LaBarbera Whites at Columbia Records. The A&R (artist and repertoire) representative offered to fly out from New York to Houston to watch Girl's Tyme perform at the local Jewish community center. But the night before the showcase, the girls went swimming. The day of the performance, Beyoncé had a clogged nose from her sinus condition, and the other girls were fatigued from staying up late. The girls did not sound their best and an angry Mathew stopped them mid-song, berated them for the previous evening's activities, and made them restart. This time they sounded considerably better. LaBarbera Whites wanted to sign the girls on the spot, but against all odds, Columbia Records and Elektra's Silent Partner Productions both presented the group with contracts. Mathew told the girls to leave the choice up to his judgment and they agreed. Mathew accepted Elektra's offer, not knowing, of course, that eight months from then, Girl's Tyme would be dropped by the company and the group would again become a free agent. For the girls, the disappointment and frustration would remind them again of *Star Search*.

A SECOND CHANCE

Before the other shoe dropped, however, Beyoncé and her colleagues moved to Atlanta, where Silent Partner was located. One of the girls' mothers chaperoned, and the group bunked in the basement of Daryl Simmons's assistant. The girls were tutored in the mornings, then spent the afternoons at the studio. Paid $150 per week, they spent their salaries mainly on weekend jaunts to malls. "We were kids, but suddenly we thought we were cool and grown up," Beyoncé said.[11]

The girls loved the independence and sense of freedom until a letter arrived one day in 1995 from Elektra. They were fired—the label had decided not to back the group any longer—a common practice in the industry when finite amounts of money force tough decisions. The group pouted for a few weeks during which Mathew delivered daily pep talks and Tina suggested going out and doing something positive. As a result, the group's confidence level rose, and the pain lessened. Still, the girls now had time to reevaluate their performance skills more critically. Beyoncé concluded the group had failed on *Star Search* and with Elektra because the girls were not yet sufficiently prepared. Beyoncé felt their vocals were not as disciplined as they could be. "We were good, but we weren't great," Beyoncé said.[12] She felt it was because they had not yet maximized their talents and needed to polish their vocal skills more.

Meanwhile, a consistently upbeat Mathew vowed to get the group another record showcase and made good on that promise. While the girls resumed practicing, Mathew returned to Columbia Records and met with Teresa LaBarbera Whites. A fellow Texan, LaBarbera Whites traveled constantly, looking for groups, bands, and singers, which was how she had spotted Girl's Tyme in the first place. But now, a year and two contracts later, it was Mathew who contacted her. LaBarbera Whites agreed to give Girl's Tyme a second chance, but this time, the group had to audition in New York City. The audition took place in a tiny conference room in the Sony building. A number of men and women—of different ethnicities and races—huddled nearby while the girls performed. "It felt too intimate—being that close and having to make eye contact was very scary," Beyoncé said.[13] The group felt tense because the girls knew this was the last chance, and if they did not turn in a top-flight performance, there might not be any more chances. They sang "Are You Ready?" and "Ain't No Sunshine" a cappella. For some reason, no one could interpret the reactions of the record executives. So the group returned to Houston clueless. The answer would be life-changing, no matter what. As soon as Girl's Tyme departed for Houston, LaBarbera Whites began trying to convince Columbia's decision makers to sign the group.

THE BIRTH OF DESTINY'S CHILD

The day the decision arrived via mail, Tina and Mathew decided to tease the girls a little. They placed the Columbia letter in an envelope bearing the letterhead of Luby's, a nationally franchised cafeteria. Girl's Tyme was at Headliners Hair Salon when Beyoncé was handed the envelope. She figured she was being given a gift certificate to eat at the cafeteria, but when she saw it was an offer of a recording contract, she and the other girls began to yell and scream. They stood in the middle of the salon surrounded by a dozen or so women under noisy dryers, and no one except Tina and Mathew knew why the girls were rejoicing.

The year was 1996, and Beyoncé was barely 15. Suddenly her world was turned topsy-turvy. Girl's Tyme was renamed Destiny's Child, and after what seemed a lifetime, Beyoncé, her father Mathew, and the other girls had finally received validation. Tina called it an exciting time since the recording deal meant the girls would finally get to fulfill lifetime goals. Everyone was thrilled, but money had no bearing on their excitement because the important thing was that the industry had judged the girls talented and had welcomed them into the elite membership of recording artists. Destiny's Child was on its way.

ON THE LAUNCH PAD

LaBarbera Whites, who first met Beyoncé and Kelly when they were nine and ten years old, respectively, knew that for Destiny's Child to succeed, the selection of songs would be critical and the musical lineup had to be age appropriate. Beyoncé and the other girls had not done a lot of song composition, so LaBarbera Whites and others scouted out material. "Kiddie songs" were eliminated as too juvenile, but in 1996 the pop tune stockpile did not have as comprehensive an inventory of teen music as it does currently. So shopping around for music consumed a lot of LaBarbera Whites's time until the second album, *The Writing's on the Wall*, when Beyoncé began writing songs that dealt with teen subjects like guys and fidelity. Then, LaBarbera Whites linked the group up with collaborators and producers. But Kelly and Beyoncé had barely entered their teens when Columbia signed them and the group's first record came out. "I literally watched them grow up," LaBarbera Whites said.[14] (LaBarbera Whites also eased the way for Jessica Simpson.) Her experience with Beyoncé and Destiny's Child was joyful right from the start. "I've watched her blossom into an amazing writer and producer," she said.[15]

As an A&R representative, LaBarbera Whites's worth to the company was measured in the final product: Did the artist and label turn out an album the public wanted to hear? Mathew's view of the entertainment industry was even more pragmatic: Everyone in music needed to think business first; otherwise, they would fail. "Music is important, but you're doing the imaging, the marketing, the promotions, all in sync," he said.[16] For instance, Mathew marketed Destiny's Child as 17-year-olds when the girls were only 15 because he felt the market response was low at that time for younger teens, so he supplied consumers with a product for older teens. His problem-solving response reflected his inherently practical business philosophy. In some ways, marketing accelerated the group's development and Beyoncé learned to be more philosophical about failures. She acknowledged that mistakes were challenges forcing personal growth. "Life is about taking missteps, tripping, falling, dusting yourself off, getting back up, and working harder to get further than where you were in the first place."[17] Beyoncé put that philosophy into concrete terms as Destiny's Child's most memorable personality and talent. She surmounted obstacles in her path and learned to avoid others. Her determination and fortitude would be tested time and again, but her faith in family and a Supreme Being would help her emerge a stronger and wiser person.

NOTES

1. Quoted in Beyoncé Knowles, Kelly Rowland, and Michelle Williams, *Soul Survivors: The Official Autobiography of Destiny's Child* (New York: Regan Books/HarperCollins, 2002), 72.

2. Quoted in Warner Roberts, "Tina Knowles: Pop Star's Mom Sews Some Diva-licious Threads," *H Texas Online*, September 2007, www. htexasonline.com (accessed April 28, 2008).

3. Kierna Mayo, "Beyoncé Unwrapped," *Teen Hollywood*, August 10, 2003, www.teenhollywood.com (accessed July 15, 2008).

4. Quoted in Knowles et al., 74.

5. Ibid.

6. Quoted in Mayo.

7. Quoted in "Destiny's Child: The New Supremes?" *Business Wire*, January 5, 2001, www.findarticles.com (accessed April 28, 2008).

8. Quoted by Marlo Cobb, "Child of Fate." *Houston Press*, March 12, 1998, www.infoseek.newsbank.com (accessed April 28, 2008).

9. Quoted in www.Brewer-international.com (accessed April 28, 2008).

10. www.Brewer-international.com (accessed April 28, 2008).

11. "LaTavia and LeToya," April 15, 2002, //mbdirt.com (accessed April 28, 2008).

12. Quoted in Richard Harrington, "Spotlight—Destiny Child's Growing Pains," *Washington Post*, September 15, 2000, N17.

13. Quoted in Knowles et al., 85.

14. Quoted by Jayne Moore, "Top A&R Exec Teresa LaBarbera Whites . . . Great Run at Sony," *SingerUniverse Magazine*, www.singeruniverse.com (accessed April 28, 2008).

15. Quoted by Moore.

16. Quoted by Rob Hochschild, "Toughing It Out," *Berklee News*, March 12, 2003, www.berkleenews.edu (accessed April 28, 2008).

17. Quoted in Knowles et al., 72–73.

Chapter 4

DESTINY'S CHILD TRIUMPHS

In 1996, Destiny's Child landed that all-important first record contract, and, as it is said, the rest is history. Over the next few years, Beyoncé went from a fresh-faced teenager who started dancing in stilettos at age 12 to a young composer who wrote and recorded 43 songs for Columbia Records in just 12 days.

Beyoncé vividly remembered the day in 1998 when Destiny's Child's first single, "No, No, No," was released. Driving back in Beyoncé's Ford Explorer from a rehearsal in Houston, she and Kelly stopped at Solange's school to wrap up the day's carpool duties. Their radio was tuned to 97.9 FM. When the two girls heard the opening bars of their soon-to-be solid-gold hit, they whooped for joy and turned the volume to max, and naturally they sang along.

NO, NO, NO

In a few weeks, thousands of Destiny's Child's fans were singing along, too. "No, No, No" was catchy, but that was not the entire reason that it flew to the top of *Billboard*'s Top 10 Singles. Originally the tempo of the song was much slower, but the day Beyoncé recorded the chorus, producer Wyclef Jean told her to speed up the recording session—it was costing too much in studio time. So Beyoncé rushed through the lyrics, and Wyclef loved the results. "And he was right—it was hot!" Beyoncé wrote.[1] Wyclef Jean helped produce Destiny's Child's self-named first album because he saw the group's potential and future longevity. "In the line of work we are in, you can see who's gonna blow and who's not gonna blow," he said.[2]

What he most respected about Beyoncé and Kelly was their humility and laid-back attitude, and he believed people with that mindset achieved long-term success in the entertainment industry.

With the huge success of "No, No, No," Beyoncé could not help but congratulate herself, but it took Tina only five minutes to thrust Beyoncé out of the limelight and back into the real world. Ironically, Tina and Beyoncé were in a record store when mom made her move. She wanted to get Beyoncé's attention, but the teen was busy and ignored her mother. That was the last time Beyoncé pulled that stunt. Tina did not mince words—she slapped Beyoncé and retorted: "You better listen to me when I talk to you. Don't think you can do that now that you got a number one song."[3] Beyoncé was embarrassed and shocked over Tina's reprimand because her parents had never even spanked her before. In hindsight she felt her mother did the right thing, for from then on, Beyoncé never took herself and her accomplishments that seriously—she abandoned any airs of self-importance.

MIRROR, MIRROR

A few months after the group signed its contract in 1996, Columbia Records decided to rework Destiny's Child's image. The plan was to tweak it here, tweak it there—making changes to outfits and makeup. The so-called trendy modifications wound up conflicting with Destiny's Child's group perception. Besides, the girls did not feel comfortable with their "new and improved" appearances because the changes did not reflect individual personality strengths and weaknesses. For instance, the label did not understand Beyoncé's natural tendency to be quiet and ordered her to talk more, ignoring her affability.

Fortunately, Tina intervened before a Spring 1998, MTV appearance and recostumed the group in Army fatigue wear. Each girl's outfit varied and was either shorts, a skirt, overalls, or baggy pants. Tina knew how to combine personality and consistency to make a statement and create an image, and she also talked Kelly into highlighting her hair with red streaks. After the MTV success, Tina took over permanently as group stylist.

THE FIRST ALBUM

Before "No, No, No" was released, Destiny's Child contributed to the movie soundtrack for *Men in Black* (1997) starring Tommy Lee Jones and Will Smith by recording the song, "Killing Time." When Beyoncé finally met co-star Will Smith at the end of a movie publicity event, his laid-back, friendly attitude impressed her. Although he was noticeably tired, he did not rush the conversation; instead, his polite, extroverted demeanor put the girls instantly at ease.

By 1999, Destiny's Child's first album was released. A blend of fast tempo songs and romantic ballads, the album registered acceptable sales numbers as a result of national and European tours. The track, "My Time Has Come," served as tribute to Destiny's Child's former manager, Andretta Tillman, who died of lupus in 1997. Beyoncé wrote only 3 of the 13 songs on the album, but even those tracks explored mature themes such as romantic deceit and unfaithful men. Despite Beyoncé's relative inexperience with the opposite sex, she zeroed in on issues that resonated with many women and young girls. The source of many of her ideas was eavesdropping on conversations in Headliners Hair Salon in Houston.

Beyoncé quickly learned that producing a hit album was not just about raw talent, universal themes, and a unique image; artistic development was key, too, so Beyoncé endeavored to transform herself into a well-rounded artist. With that goal in mind, she turned to production experts such as Master P, Jermaine Dupri, and Dwayne Wiggins, and gradually she became adept at the behind-the-scenes creative work.

Another "first" was Destiny's Child's performance on *VH1's Divas* with Diana Ross. The group talked to Ross for about a half-hour, and she wished them the same life-changing experiences she had enjoyed, inviting them to contact her if they needed further advice. Beyoncé also saw Mariah Carey at the divas tribute—another role model of Beyoncé's—and she actually shed tears of excitement because just the year before, when the girls had watched *Divas Live,* Beyoncé had prayed for a day when Destiny's Child would appear on that show.

DESTINY'S SECOND CHILD

More good news awaited them after the 1999 release of their second album, *The Writing's on the Wall.* After the first album came out, the girls thoroughly critiqued it, listing both good and bad features, and then used those points to determine content for a second album. In contrast to the debut album, Beyoncé wrote 11 of the 14 songs, and the themes focused on relationships with the opposite sex, for example, challenging a boyfriend to say his girl's name on the phone ("Say My Name") and chastising guys interested only in a girl's money ("Bills, Bills, Bills").

She'kspere, known for his unique sound, produced the album in collaboration with Kandi, a talented song writer from Xscape, and producer

Rodney Jerkins contributed to the fast-paced "Say My Name." The album encouraged women to be independent from their boyfriends, husbands, or parents, but the group took heat for some of the lyrics, especially the line in the song "Bills, Bills, Bills:" "You trifling, good-for-nothing-type of brother." Although Beyoncé explained the line applied to both genders, as anyone could shift personal financial responsibility to a lover, men angered by what they perceived as accusations might have boycotted the album. But they did not and the album sold more than nine million copies worldwide.[4] Kelly summed up the reasons for the album's popularity as "fast unforgettable lyrics that delivered a party feeling"[5] and credited Beyoncé for the "in your face" vocals and good harmonies.[6]

The phenomenal success of *The Writing's on the Wall* led to offers of modeling, movie contracts, and joint assignments with high-profile performers such as Jada Pinkett, Sisters with Voices, Heavy D., Sean "Puffy" Combs, Maxwell, and Mary J. Blige. At last the girls' dreams were coming true.

THEN THERE WERE TWO

Beyoncé's enthusiasm gradually dissipated, but it had nothing to do with burnout. By late 1999, tensions peaked within Destiny's Child. Competition and squabbles over money finally brought longstanding hostilities to the surface. LaTavia and LeToya filed a law suit against Mathew, a legal move that made reconciliation virtually impossible. Although fans were shocked and dismayed when the legal action was aired publicly, Beyoncé recognized that negative emotions had brewed for a while and the members had moved in different directions. Still, Beyoncé regretted losing two good friends.

So in 1999 in a last attempt to repair the damage, the four women sought counsel with their youth minister at Saint John's United Methodist Church, the Houston church they regularly attended. They still could not resolve their differences because of an accumulation of grievances, and this disturbed the acknowledged "peacemaker"—Beyoncé—who had always subscribed to the motto, "Let's work it out." She disliked drama, tending to empathize with the person in pain, but Beyoncé was hard pressed to cope with the current emotional upheaval. She was caught in the middle between love and loyalty for her father and the camaraderie and shared respect of friends.

Now officially plaintiffs, LeToya and LaTavia accused Mathew, their former manager, of "greed, insistence on control, self-dealing, and promotion of his daughter's interests at (their) expense."[7] Basically, the two teens fired Mathew because of breach of partnership and fiduciary duties and failed negotiations resulting from threats and intimidation. Beyoncé was hurt twice by the lawsuit; the first time, because two close friends with whom she had cried and laughed now accused her father of nepotism and thievery, and the second time, because some of Beyoncé's fans blamed her for the group's schism. Internet chat groups and Web sites rumbled with mean-spirited accusations, and fans at airports, hotels, and other public places spewed lies and spread malicious gossip. "It was hard then. I'm not even gonna say it wasn't," she said.[8]

The conflict persisted because LeToya and LaTavia sued Beyoncé for defamation. Beyoncé felt extremely hurt by this legal maneuver, and Beyoncé's father also took it badly, which exacerbated her pain. She and Mathew had always regarded Destiny's Child as a family united in love, but clearly, the feeling was not reciprocated. Between the combined stress of legal fireworks, the negative feedback from her audience, and the hate e-mail, Beyoncé developed acne for the first time and fell into a depression, retreating to her bedroom and brooding for days.[9]

The legal fight also stripped Beyoncé of her naiveté, which probably did her a favor. In the beginning, her response to criticism from fans and audiences was to lead everyone in prayer, but as she matured, she became more thick-skinned and self-protective. She recognized viciousness in certain people, so instead of reverting to her customary tried-and-true Pollyanna attitude, she allowed her alter ego Sasha to emerge at show time and absorb the blows. "It's a good way to keep sane," she said.[10]

Ironically, the lawsuits and malicious conversations stirred up media attention and Destiny's Child sold even more records. Beyoncé realized she was reaping enormous dividends from the animosity of fans. "Controversy sells albums," Beyoncé said. But "if we didn't have the talent to back up the drama, we wouldn't be here."[11]

YOU DO THE MATH

As Beyoncé and Kelly struggled to keep their careers afloat, Mathew denied LaTavia and LeToya's demands for independent managers to represent them during negotiations. Within days after legal papers were filed in 2000, Mathew fired LaTavia and LeToya, which triggered giant problems for Destiny's Child's performance schedule, as the group's commitments were made under the assumption that four members, not two, would perform. Beyoncé was scared by the defection of LeToya and LaTavia, but refused to cancel any appearances, so Kelly and she sometimes performed alone.

Another challenge arose with the videotaping of the song "Say My Name." Everything had been choreographed and arranged for four vocalists and dancers, so Mathew reacted quickly and hired two replacements—Michelle Williams and Farrah Franklin. The newcomers learned the dance steps, but lip synched the lyrics because LeToya and LaTavia had already recorded the track. Despite their status as newcomers, Michelle and Farrah took on heavy weekly schedules—live radio interviews, MTV video sessions, and other promotional activities. Meanwhile, rehearsals for an Australian tour went into high gear and Franklin missed several practices. At first, Beyoncé made excuses for Farrah, emphasizing her inexperience and the new burden of a time-intensive schedule. It wasn't until the actual day of their flight to Australia that Beyoncé, Michelle, and Kelly realized that Franklin did not intend to fulfill her obligations. During a last-minute telephone call, Beyoncé told Franklin it was unprofessional to renege on her promise.[12]

That was exactly what Franklin did, however, and the foursome dwindled to a trio. Beyoncé worried immediately about the rechoreographing of dance moves and the rearrangement of vocal parts that a smaller group necessitated, but the three girls soon discovered that less was more. Beyoncé recognized that Michelle and Kelly sang backup better than ever, and an a cappella gospel medley did not require an extra vocalist after all. Destiny's Child had achieved 100 percent success with four members, but now three could get the job done just as well.

Like her idol Madonna, Beyoncé reinvented Destiny's Child and the total effect was positive. The vocals became tighter and stronger, which enhanced the performance. "We're spiritually better, and mentally everybody's supportive of each other," Beyoncé said.[13] She felt calmer now that a fully cooperative, interdependent group replaced a dysfunctional one, and her philosophy shifted from an apprehensive let's-hope-we-can-get-through-this-one to the solid belief that out of a messy situation, a healthier future had emerged.

SURVIVING

After returning from Australia in 2000, Destiny's Child produced a portion of the soundtrack for the hit film *Charlie's Angels*. "Independent Women Part I," on *The Writing's on the Wall* (the second album), climbed the charts quickly, becoming a cash cow for the group and Beyoncé followed up on this achievement almost immediately and composed songs for the group's third album, *Survivor*. Because she was still reacting to the turmoil that had ravaged Destiny's Child, Beyoncé took inspiration for the new album from a teasing on-air remark made by a radio disc jockey. He said Destiny's Child was like the television show *Survivor*: "You had to guess which member would be out next."[14] Instead of becoming furious, Beyoncé sublimated the situation and channeled it into the creative act of musical composition.

It took Beyoncé only five minutes to write "Survivor" and she was nervous about the song until she got feedback. Her two colleagues raved about the chorus, certain the song would be a hit, and this optimism pervaded the studio environment since "Survivor" had kicked off the first recording session. Another track, "The Story of Beauty," which appeared on the new album, told the tale of a sexually abused child who confided her story in a letter to Destiny's Child. The lyrics implored the child not to cry but instead believe in her self-worth and beauty.

BACK TO THE FUTURE

In October 2000, Destiny's Child revisited a time when the group's self-worth had diminished: The girls appeared on Ed McMahon's *Next Big Star* television special, a talent contest that started out as an Internet competition at www.nextbigstar.com in the categories of comedy, dance, kid's music, and theatrical music. People viewed each contestant's talent video online and visitors to the site voted for the contestants they deemed best; finalists appeared on the TV special along with Destiny's Child. In one of life's little ironies, Destiny's Child ended up returning to Orlando, Florida—the site of their *Star Search* loss—to perform on another Ed McMahon-hosted show. On this occasion, the group had a much more rewarding outcome.

WINNERS

The rest of 2000 was just as inspiring. In the fall the group released a holiday album, *8 Days of Christmas*, and performed on NBC's *Christmas in Rockefeller Center* program. Then in January 2001, the group received an invitation to sing at President Bush's inauguration. "I never thought that I would meet—let alone perform for—the president of our country," Beyoncé said. She enjoyed the informality of sitting around, chatting with the president, and knowing he came from her home state.[15]

Before the show, however, catastrophe struck when the costumes were lost and Tina hurried out to buy new outfits. Security refused to allow her back in to the White House, and the three teens had to make due with what they were wearing, which were only T-shirts and pants. Being young, inventive—and desperate—Beyoncé, Kelly, and Michelle cut up their clothes and put everything back together imaginatively with safety pins. Fortunately, the audience loved the group's outfits and no one caught on to the technical blunder.

This near-disaster turned out to be a warm-up for the 2000 *Grammys* held in February 2001, when the group planned to sing a medley. Right before Destiny's Child's entrance that evening, Beyoncé—usually calm, cool, and collected (at least once Sasha took over)—could not remember her moves and vocals. "I can say that night was the most nervous I have ever been in my life," Beyoncé wrote.[16] Two reasons for her discomfiture were that the group had been nominated for five Grammys and Madonna was sitting front and center. To make matters worse, Beyoncé thought her fellow musicians were scoffing at the idea of a five-Grammy win for Destiny's Child. Instead, Destiny's Child received a standing ovation and praise from such celebrities as Gloria Estefan, Shakira, Sir Elton John, and Bono.

The highlight of the year was winning the 2001 Songwriter of the Year award from the American Society of Composers, Authors, and Publishers (ASCAP) at the Pop Music Awards. The first black woman and the second female ever to win the award, Beyoncé dissolved into tears and was left speechless at the podium. "I didn't even have time to thank everyone—I needed to hurry backstage and find a box of Kleenex!"[17]

OPENING UP EMOTIONALLY

Beyoncé's emotional meltdown in front of millions of Grammy viewers presaged more openness and honesty in her songwriting. For example, after gaining a few extra pounds, she felt public pressure to lose weight, so the song "Bootylicious," which referred to her rear end, emerged from her frustration over the "weight debate." The song "Happy Face" grew out of her need to fake happiness after the breakup of the original Destiny's Child. Her biggest hits seemed to result from personal experiences revealing intense anger, happiness, or sadness that she opted to share with her audience. For Beyoncé, writing and recording songs was cathartic—a therapy-like activity that she used to unburden herself of negative emotions and energy.

Beyoncé's career commitments helped her cope during the days after 9/11, when the country mourned the nearly 4,000 Americans killed in terrorist attacks on the New York World Trade Center and the Pentagon. Beyoncé sang the song "Survivor" at benefit concerts in New York City and Washington, D.C., where the goal was to raise funds for survivors and honor the friends and families of those who perished. Destiny's Child empathized with the audience's pain, and the group's shared strength and courage helped them deal with the sadness and sense of loss. "They (the audience) were crying and holding up pictures and big pieces of paper that said 'I miss you,'" Kelly said.[18]

In spite of the threat of further domestic terrorism, Beyoncé enjoyed the best time in her life. At long last, she was an acclaimed songwriter and singer and her self-esteem had rocketed to new heights. She had met every challenge—good and bad—and learned the emotional ABCs that home schooling and tutoring had omitted from her education: She discovered that self-love and acceptance enabled one to stop caring what others thought and she could more easily live now with her mistakes. She also realized that criticism from other people was more about them—their jealousy or sadness, for example—than about her. "It takes going through this to realize that's how life is," she said.[19] Most important, Beyoncé recognized that it was time for her to create new dreams, to expand her horizons and aim for different goals. She was ready to risk the role of solo entertainer because she felt certain that confidence and a constellation of talents and abilities were on her side. "You can accomplish anything in life," Beyoncé said, "if you work hard."[20]

NOTES

1. Beyoncé Knowles, Kelly Rowland, and Michelle Williams, *Soul Survivors: The Official Autobiography of Destiny's Child* (New York: Regan Books/HarperCollins, 2002), 89.

2. Sarah Benzuly, "Wyclef Jean," *Mix*, August 1, 2003, www.mixonline.com/recording/interviews/audio_wyclef_jean/ (accessed May 1, 2008).

3. Quoted in "Beyoncé Knowles' Different Destiny," www.ivillage.co.uk. (accessed April 30, 2008).

4. "Destiny's Child," www.netmusiccountdown.com (accessed January 14, 2009).

5. Knowles et al., 90.

6. Hector Saldana, "Four Young Texas Singers Fulfilling Their Destiny," *San Antonio Express-News*, Dec. 3, 1999, www.infoseek.newsbank.com (accessed April 30, 2008).

7. Knowles et al., 96.

8. Quoted by Alona Wartofsky, "A Child of Destiny—Beyoncé Knowles Is Growing into a Renaissance Woman," *Washington Post*, September 23, 2003, www.infoseek.newsbank.com (accessed April 30, 2008).

9. Knowles et al., 99.

10. Quoted in "Beyoncé the Ice Princess," *Blender*, October 2006, www.blender.com (accessed June 6, 2008).

11. Quoted in Jon Bream, "Behind the Music—They've Had Enough Conflict for a VH1 Special, But Destiny's Child Keeps Jumpin', Jumpin' Up the Charts," *Minneapolis Star Tribune*, September 8, 2000, www.infoseek.newsbank.com (accessed April 30, 2008).

12. Knowles et al., 3.

13. Richard Harrington, "Spotlight—Destiny Child's Growing Pains," *Washington Post*, September 15, 2000, N17.

14. Quoted in Chris Patrick, *Beyoncé & Destiny's Child* (New York: Scholastic, 2005), 22.

15. Knowles et al., 140–141.

16. Knowles et al., 149.

17. Knowles et al., 150.

18. Knowles et al., 225.

19. Quoted by Jevaillier Jefferson, "The Big Break That Launched My Career," *Black Collegian Online*, 2003, www.blackcollegian.com (accessed May 8, 2008).

20. Quoted by Shelly Ann Richmond, "Born to Sing," *Scholastic Action*, December 11, 2006, www.ebscohost.com (accessed April 30, 2008).

Chapter 5

FLYING SOLO

Whether Beyoncé knew it or not, she desperately wanted to challenge herself in another medium and expand her repertoire of musical accomplishments. She also wanted independence and the freedom that it brought, so film was the logical choice for her, especially after MTV asked her in 2001 to star in *Carmen: a Hip-Hopera*, a modern hip-hop version of Bizet's classic opera. Ironically the role of Carmen was characterized by a deviousness that went beyond anything that Beyoncé had yet experienced. Beyoncé's own personality was easily a polar opposite; whereas Carmen was manipulative, Beyoncé was straightforward and almost always the quintessential nice girl. The reverse casting complicated Beyoncé's portrayal, for the young singer had difficulty fathoming the degree of evil intent implicit in the role of Carmen.

To make the part of Carmen more palatable, the director agreed to flesh out the cold-blooded femme fatale with a few redeeming features. Changes in characterization and setting (modern-day Philadelphia instead of nineteenth-century Spain) notwithstanding, Beyoncé still had to convey the desperate and diabolical machinations behind a flagrantly sexual woman and her doomed love affair with a modern-day corrupt cop who planted drugs on an innocent boy.

CARMEN

As a novice actress, Beyoncé reverted to type when preparing for the role of Carmen, which meant summoning forth her perfectionistic tendencies so she could learn as much as possible about acting in 12 weeks.

The good thing about the compressed filming schedule was that it tested her independence in a relatively safe environment, allowed her to discuss issues with the producers and the MTV staff, and, for the first time, transformed her into a business person. "Suddenly I was making up my own mind and learning to trust my judgment," Beyoncé wrote.[1]

The most difficult hurdles for her were press interviews because as the most visible member of Destiny's Child, she had perfected the art of functioning within a group setting, but not as an individual. She realized she was no longer in that comfort zone when interview questions started probing personal areas of her life. "I learned something about myself outside of Destiny's Child," Beyoncé said. "Movies are my college, my time to go and discover."[2] As a member of Destiny's Child, Beyoncé learned that the techniques of compromise and negotiation allowed her to survive in a group environment, but now she needed to develop an entirely different set of social skills. For the first time, she began to understand the concept of autonomy and to separate her needs, wants, and desires from those of Destiny's Child. It turned into a far liberating, but more solitary, experience, and to offset feelings of detachment and physical as well as psychological distance from her partners, Beyoncé made friendships on the set with members of the cast and crew. She forced herself to communicate with people in an honest, open way, and it had the cumulative effect of improving her acting as well as her self-esteem. Best of all, Beyoncé received kudos for her dramatic portrayal of Carmen from theater critics, who said she turned in a "scintillating performance";[3] praised her "surplus of star power";[4] and said she "shines in the musical numbers."[5] Even the New York Times agreed the role of Carmen was "vividly played."[6]

SECOND ACT: FOXXY CLEOPATRA

Beyoncé's auspicious 2002 debut in Carmen did not go unnoticed, and the result was an offer of another Hollywood script, this time the role of Foxxy Cleopatra in the third feature film of the Austin Powers series: Goldmember. The role required more acting than singing, which gave Beyoncé second thoughts, but producer John Lyons, who had praised Beyoncé in Carmen, believed the singer could turn in a convincing performance as a 1970s secret agent. Nevertheless Beyoncé was nervous when she auditioned with comedian and film star Mike Meyers, who tried to alleviate her anxiety with jokes and impressions. Beyoncé, however, was so intimidated by the audition and hiring process that she brought her mother along and allowed her to negotiate with director Jay Roach and others. Beyoncé thought she made a fatal error when the producer asked her reaction to taking on a comedy role because she blurted out that she was not sure she was up to the challenge. She immediately realized, "That's probably not what you should tell a Hollywood producer thinking about casting you in their multimillion-dollar comedy," Beyoncé wrote.[7] Her second audition with comedian Mike Meyers went better because she really proved she wanted the part and was able to convince other people. Dressed in a cat suit and Afro wig á la 1960s actress Pam Grier, Beyoncé demonstrated her knowledge of and affection for the 1970s and the black power movement, wearing funky clothes and using hip language. Despite reservations about her acting technique, Beyoncé acquiesced to the $3 million movie offer and relocated to Hollywood and an apartment near Beverly Hills.

Preparation was difficult for the singer and although she memorized her lines well, feelings of inferiority plagued her. Her self-criticism exacerbated her discomfort and so did fears that the cast and crew might assume she was a diva and resent her. Beyoncé also worried that everyone would scoff at her motives for doing the movie and consider it the predictable agenda of an overly ambitious, avaricious pop singer. To head off criticism, she made a preemptive strike, admitting her ignorance of Hollywood jargon and the behind-the-scenes techniques. The biggest help came from enjoying the spunky, spirited dialogue of the script and the motivations associated with Foxxy's character, as well as maintaining a professional demeanor. Still, when Beyoncé was not performing, she lapsed into silence and in her free time returned to her old hobby of painting. She bought a large canvas at the local art store and experimented in one of the hardest mediums, oil paint. During filming she produced several oils, including an abstract image of a woman with an Afro.

On the release of the film, reviewers praised Beyoncé's skill at transforming Foxxy into a more tender-hearted personality[8] and acknowledged that Beyoncé "kept the movie moving."[9] Other reviewers recognized the blaxploitation aspect of Foxxy's character and thought the director should have probed that angle more. Beyoncé also recorded "Work It Out" for the movie soundtrack, and the song became a Top 10 hit in the United Kingdom and a Top 40 in the Netherlands, Australia, and Ireland. Unfortunately, U.S. disc jockeys rarely played the track and MTV Jams and VH1 Soul seldom aired the video, so the soundtrack did not catch on in the states.

THE FIGHTING TEMPTATIONS

In 2003, Beyoncé filmed *The Fighting Temptations*, playing "Lilly," a jazz singer and an unwed mother who joined a gospel choir to help the group win a singing contest. The movie, which earned Beyoncé $1.5 million and starred Cuba Gooding Jr., an actor Beyoncé long admired, combined Beyoncé's musical and acting skills. She got to sing hymns and "some really soulful, funky stuff," she said.[10] The director cast her in a kiss-ing scene—something Beyoncé disliked—but her friendship with Cuba Gooding helped ease her discomfort. She also recorded the song "Fighting Temptations" with rappers Missy Elliott, MC Lyte, and Free, but the track did not make it to the charts.

Beyoncé relished the opportunity to play a normal person with real problems and issues—not a glamour girl—and when one of the screen-writers wanted to eliminate Lilly's illegitimate child from the plot, Be-yoncé objected. She loved Lily's complex struggle to raise her son without his father and turn him into an upstanding citizen. Another attraction was that the film had an ensemble cast and not just one or two big stars. Beyoncé wanted to perfect her acting skills because she anticipated be-coming a force in the industry, so achieving mediocrity was not an option. An ensemble project would provide the opportunity to learn as much as possible from director Jonathan Lynn, her co-actors, and the production staff. Beyoncé even asked Lynn to assist her in her learning curve by con-tinuing to film scenes until she delivered the emotion or body language the film required—a strategy she hoped would help her master her new craft. Some reviewers were less than enthusiastic about Beyoncé's perfor-mance as Lilly, but well-known movie critic Roger Ebert acknowledged Beyoncé's potential to go beyond playing only sexy, glamorous parts.

THE PINK PANTHER

The filming of The Pink Panther in 2006 with Steve Martin and Kevin Kline took place during a three-week vacation break in Beyoncé's sched-ule and was a revival of and prequel to the old Panther movies of the 1970s and 1980s starring Peter Sellers.

Beyoncé, who played the pop culture character Xania, an international superstar, wanted to learn from the best so she was genuinely pleased to work with two experienced and respected actors. The role was far from a stretch, but Beyoncé did have at least one challenge: to keep a straight face during scenes with comic actor Steve Martin. Her professional atti-tude, especially her dislike for wasted time, enabled her to get through the filming without dissolving into hysterics.

Most reviewers panned the movie, for example, claiming Beyoncé was nothing more than "eye-candy" and an "excuse for a pop single."[11] Re-gardless, both The Pink Panther and Austin Powers: Goldmember opened at Number 1 in the box office, grossing over $481,364,728 worldwide.[12] The song "Check on It," which Beyoncé wrote for the soundtrack, raced up the charts to Number 1, becoming Beyoncé's first hit song from a movie. The one time Beyoncé actually viewed the entire film was on a plane, where not too many people recognized her as the Afro-wearing Foxxy character in the movie since by then she wore a completely different hairstyle. But Beyoncé wrote, "There was this little boy sitting next to me with his dad and he was like, 'Dad, that's Foxxy Cleopatra!' And everybody on the plane was turning around"[13] to Beyoncé's embarrassment.

DREAMGIRLS

In some respects Beyoncé had prepared for the film *Dreamgirls* her whole life because of Tina's passion for the Supremes and that group's influence on Beyoncé's vocal style and presentation. Based on the hit Broadway musical of the same name, the movie *Dreamgirls* followed the rise of an all-girl Motown group of the 1960s, the Dreams, and its eventual breakup. Deena (Beyoncé's role) was loosely based on music legend Diana Ross, and other cast members included Jamie Foxx, Eddie Murphy, and American Idol contestant Jennifer Hudson. Beyoncé's role presented a challenge and an opportunity to mature in acting skills and avoid being typecast as a sex object or a passive, needy woman. Because the role emphasized acting rather than singing, she prepared by rehearsing with a drama coach, who helped her show Deena's pain and disappointment. Beyoncé also endeavored to show Deena's personality through her appearance: full makeup, big hair, glamorous dresses, and matching shoes. Beyoncé studied tapes of Diana Ross's performances and interviews, which helped her mimic Ross's hand gestures and eyelash fluttering and motivated Beyoncé to lose 20 pounds using an unconventional diet of warm lemonade, maple syrup, and cayenne powder. (Beyoncé later admitted on a British television show that she did not recommend the diet, which was based on the book *The Master Cleanser*.) Beyoncé's total makeover helped her morph into one of the sophisticated, ladylike "Dreams."

Although Beyoncé admired Diana Ross ("I met her and she was very nice, which made me feel great," Beyoncé said[14]), reporters annoyed Beyoncé with repeated comparisons between Destiny's Child and the Supremes, although Beyoncé and Ross had dissimilar personalities. For example, the Deena/Ross character exhibited less control than Beyoncé did and unlike Ross, Beyoncé wrote and produced her own records and did not hire people to scout out prospective hits. Also, Destiny's Child never grew up in Detroit's black ghetto; the members were middle-class Texans. Before *Dreamgirls* was released to critical acclaim in the United

States in November 2006, a 30-minute clip was viewed in May of that year at the Cannes Film Festival on the French Riviera. Beyoncé won a Golden Globe nomination for Best Actress in a Comedy or Musical. "It was the role of a lifetime," she said.[15] The experience fueled Beyoncé's confidence, and she vowed from then on to act in a movie every year.

GOING IT ALONE

Dreamgirls was a lot to bite off; Beyoncé had just gone solo as a singer after years of turning down offers from several record labels. During the late 1990s, she wanted to perform in a group, but based on her talent and vitality, it was inevitable she would later crave the recognition and remuneration only a solo act could provide. Still, she knew that leaving the comfort and security of a successful Grammy-Award-winning group like Destiny's Child could prove disastrous. She remembered Dawn Robinson's fate after leaving En Vogue (a 1980s girl group that influenced Destiny's Child). Robinson never achieved further success because her solo album, *You Will Never*, received little airplay or promotion from the record company and failed to climb the charts. Another example of "has-been" solo singers included Philippe Wynn, who started with the Spinners, then left and sank to oblivion. Also, Beyoncé weighed the possibility that her departure from Destiny's Child might mean the group would disband. This had happened to Diana Ross and the Supremes as well as to Lionel Richie and the Commodores. On the other hand, Beyoncé recalled success stories from artists like Patti LaBelle, Dave Hollister (BLACKstreet), and Anita Baker (formerly with Chapter 8). Another consideration was Beyoncé's "mothering" tendency since she played an important nurturing role in the group. Although the three members complemented each other's personalities, Beyoncé brought out the best in everyone and steered them in the right direction. What would happen if she left them?

SELF-EXPLORATION

The lure and excitement of self-exploration won out, however, and Beyoncé reveled in the anticipation of many "firsts," including a solo album and solo tour. After filming *Carmen* and gaining further self-insight, Beyoncé realized she wanted her music to express her new self-discoveries and deviate from Destiny's Child's trademark style of hooks, aggressive lyrics, and hip-hop beat. As a result, Beyoncé avoided traditional R&B, and her scope of composition expanded when she recorded her first soul album in the style of Aretha Franklin and James Brown. She integrated live instruments and innovative chord changes into introspective ballads that resembled a personal journal. She also used new producers: "There are so many great people working out of their basements who are hungry," she said. "You don't want your stuff to sound like everybody else's."[16]

That vision evolved into the album *Dangerously in Love*, which was released in 2003 and went platinum within a month, soaring to the top of the charts in the United Kingdom, Canada, Australia, the Netherlands, Germany, Ireland, Norway, Greece, and the Philippines. The album, to which a number of pop musicians contributed (including Missy Elliot, Sean Paul, Mario Winans, Big Boi, Luther Vandross, and Jay-Z) offered variety: hip-hop, soul, dance music, ballads, and R&B. The mega-hit single, "Crazy in Love," quickly established a place for itself in the archives of memorable music, but the story of its origin gained equal importance.

Beyoncé and producer Rich Harrison had the melody and music to what would eventually be called "Crazy in Love," but they needed the right lyrics. One day Beyoncé walked into the studio looking a little unkempt and hassled; her clothes did not match and her hair was uncombed. "I'm looking crazy right now," Beyoncé said.[17] At that, Harrison leaped up and determined that would be the hook and began writing. Afterwards, Beyoncé still felt the song lacked something so she consulted Jay-Z, who wandered into the studio around 3 a.m., listened to the song, then mixed a little rap with traditional lyrics. Satisfied with the results, Jay-Z consulted on other pieces, advising Beyoncé on how to rewrite the verses to "Baby Boy" and convincing her of his talent. She felt Jay-Z could write for anyone—male or female—because of his extensive musical knowledge, which even included trivia such as the fact that the horn melody in "Crazy in Love" originated from a 1970 song by the Chi-Lites.

PERFECTIONISM AND PRODUCTION

Beyoncé's natural proclivity toward perfectionism plus the high expectations of fans put so much pressure on the young superstar that it sometimes interfered with her creativity and versatility. Beyoncé's self-criticism also clashed at times with her instincts, but she usually followed her gut feelings and desire to grow as a writer and vocalist. That meant wearing many hats during the production of the album *Dangerously in Love*, especially writing more personal songs. Because she no longer worried about upstaging anyone in Destiny's Child, she chose more of the content, produced selections, mixed tracks, and collaborated with other musicians. Beyoncé found it psychologically rewarding and said, "I felt free because I could go into the studio and talk about whatever I wanted."[18] And what

she wanted was to express love—how a woman experienced it and how it
weakened her defenses and increased her vulnerability to hurt and disappointment. She wanted to communicate the timelessness of love through
musical expression and get feedback from fans. That was one reason for
the hidden "Daddy" track at the album's end (dedicated to Mathew, it fol-
lows 15 blank seconds after the last song).

WEMBLEY STADIUM

To publicize *Dangerously in Love*, Beyoncé set out on her first solo European and U.K. tour in 2003 after the release of the album. The tour
started in Liverpool at the Manchester Evening News Arena, where there
was a mixed reaction to Beyoncé's performance. Although one critic raved
about Beyoncé's eye-popping, high-flying entrance in mini-skirt and bra,
the writer also said the drama was not sustained because the audience
knew only half of the songs and tracks from *Dangerously in Love* (such as
"Be with You"). This lapse prevented Beyoncé's performance from pro-
gressing to a higher level of excitement. On the other hand, Beyoncé's
vocal ability was "beyond criticism" even if as a solo performer, she lacked
for skills.[19] Beyoncé later videotaped her Wembley Stadium show and the
DVD sold well because of her unorthodox entrance by means of a har-
ness that lowered her head-first from the theater roof to the stage. Said
Beyoncé, "I saw it in a Broadway show and it looked really cool. It was ok
the first time, but when you have to do it 30 times . . ."[20]

Beyoncé experienced conflicting emotions during the tour because although she felt grateful for all the attention from her fans, she was also a
little overwhelmed by their demands, such as for autographs, letters and
photos. She had the insight, however, to realize that although her fans'
feedback was mainly positive, they sometimes demanded things, such as
kissing, that no normal human being could or would choose to respond
to. The loss of control scared her, but the tour generated lots of money,
as well as psychological benefits. "When I get on the stage I feel free,"
Beyoncé said.[21] That liberation galvanized her as did the knowledge that
her performances generated enough income for her to retire one day and
raise a family.

LADIES FIRST TOUR

Next on her spring 2004 agenda, Beyoncé signed on for The Verizon
Ladies First Tour, a 24-city trek across America with performers Missy
Elliot, Alicia Keys, and Tamia. As in her solo tour, Beyoncé made a spec-

tacular entrance, this time in a white chariot carried by four male backup dancers. Within seconds, she leaped onto the stage and belted out a number of Destiny's Child's hits, including "Baby Boy," "Say My Name," "Independent Woman," and "Survivor."

According to one critic, Beyoncé "excelled in spite of excess," with credit going to "blinding costume changes, lascivious choreography," and Beyoncé's ability to "connect" with the audience.[22] It didn't hurt that Jay-Z dropped by one time in Hartford, Connecticut, joining Beyoncé in the number "Crazy in Love." Another critic remarked on Beyoncé's "wide variety of . . . material" and her counsel to young girls in the audience that "they can do anything they want to in life."[23] Three days later in Phoenix, another reviewer compared Beyoncé and Alicia Keys, commenting that Keys established a rapport with the audience by virtue of her personality, but Beyoncé seemed on automatic pilot with little spontaneity. The critic also said Beyoncé used "vocal gymnastics," costume changes, and other "gimmicks" to appeal to the crowd despite praising Beyoncé's delivery of "Crazy in Love" as a "party-worthy version."[24]

WHERE OPERA MEETS POP

Although Beyoncé's first tour did not please all the critics, *Cove Magazine* placed her at Number 7 on the 100 Most Outstanding Pop Vocals of all time, right behind Whitney Houston, one of Beyoncé's heroes. Beyoncé also earned a mark of 48 out of a possible 50 for technical skills, and the magazine described her as a dramatic mezzo-soprano whose abilities equaled those of opera singers with three-octave ranges.[25] Beyoncé summed up her first tour in these words:

> Every moment is not perfect. But it's definitely more good times than bad. There are certain nights that you know you hit that crazy note and you know that spin went extra fast. And you look out and people are just into it and you've worked so hard and now it's paying off and you can see why you dedicated your life to this.[26]

FIVE GRAMMYS

In 2004, Beyoncé won five Grammys, making her one of the rare performers to have that distinction. Opening the awards show with Prince, Beyoncé appeared shocked and grateful to win honors and perform among such accomplished artists. Her awards included Best Contemporary R&B Album, Best R&B Song ("Crazy in Love"), and Best Female R&B Vocal Performance. She also received recognition for the July 2003 achievement of being the first and so far only female artist to have a single recording and album simultaneously top the charts in both the United States and the United Kingdom. Her Grammy acceptance speech acknowledged her pride in knowing that she was only 17 years old when she first started singing *and* producing.

REUNITED AND GOODBYE

After the Grammys, Beyoncé realized there was no returning home to the emotional and creative safety of Destiny's Child, and she needed to make a final break with the group that had catapulted her to fame and fortune. So she wrote songs for what would be Destiny's Child's last album, *Destiny Fulfilled,* which was released in November 2004. With everyone taking turns singing lead on single tracks that included "Lose My Breath" and "Soldier," the album hit Number 1 on *Billboard*'s R&B/Hip-Hop Chart and Number 2 on the *Billboard* 200. Although the album was a financial success, critics were puzzled as to why the group had produced another album considering the members' diversity of musical goals. Michelle wanted to concentrate more on gospel music, and Kelly turned to rock and edgier tunes. The music critic for the *New York Times* called *Destiny Fulfilled* "surprisingly perfunctory" and "tepid,"[27] and most critics agreed that the material contained more sexual content (Destiny's Child "feel like they can talk about stuff that before they were too young to talk about," said Rodney Jerkins, who produced "Lose My Breath." "I think that's the place they're at. It's not raunchy, but sexy."[28])

In 2005, Destiny's Child embarked on a promotional tour for the album—a lavish extravaganza that required 13 buses to carry dancers, caterers, and assorted staff—and the production traveled to more than 70 cities in Australia, Asia, Europe, and North America. Beyoncé kept everyone focused and professional; for example, when her mother began to cry in Tokyo over a costume that disappointed her, Beyoncé knew the right words to calm Tina down quickly.

By June 2005, Destiny's Child announced a final concert in Vancouver, British Columbia, which was covered by CNN and newspapers from all over the country. Critics called the performance unforgettable both technically and emotionally, and the harmonies and medleys amazed the audience. No one was too surprised when the background dancers appeared with bouquets of white flowers, which they presented to the singers. Tearfully, Beyoncé told the audience of the group's nine-year struggle to achieve their goals. "This isn't something somebody put together. This is love."[29] An era ended amid raves and waves of goodbye, and another opportunity to shine was right around the corner.

NOTES

1. Quoted in Beyoncé Knowles, Kelly Rowland, and Michelle Williams, *Soul Survivors: The Official Autobiography of Destiny's Child* (New York: Regan Books/ HarperCollins, 2002), 216.

2. Quoted in Mimi Valdes, "The Metamorphosis," *Vibe*, July 25, 2003, www. bookrags.com (accessed April 16, 2008).

3. Quoted by Kevin Filipski, *Carmen—a Hip-Hopera*, 2001, www.amazon. com (accessed April 16, 2008).

4. Quoted by Steven Oxman, *Carmen-A Hip-Hopera*, May 2, 2001, www. variety.com (accessed April 16, 2008).

5. Quoted by Kevin Laforest, *Carmen-A Hip-Hopera*, www.apolloguide.com (accessed April 16, 2008).

6. Quoted by Caryn James, "Critic's Notebook; Yo, Carmen is the Name, and a Class Act is Her Game," *The New York Times*, May 8, 2001, www.nytimes. com (accessed April 16, 2008).

7. Quoted in Knowles et al., 254.

8. Terri Dougherty, *Beyoncé* (New York: Lucent/Thomson Gale, 2007), 60–61.

9. Quoted by Ron Weiskind, "Austin Powers in Goldmember," *Pittsburgh Post-Gazette*, July 26, 2002, www.post-gazette.com (accessed April 16, 2008).

10. Quoted in Dougherty, 66.

11. Quoted by Steve Davis, "The Pink Panther," *Austin Chronicle*, Feb. 10, 2006, www.austinchronicle.com (accessed April 16, 2008).

12. "Beyoncé Knowles," www.biographicon.com (accessed September 5, 2008).

13. Quoted in Billy Johnson, "Destiny Awaits," May 27, 2004, www.music. yahoo.com (accessed April 16, 2008).

14. Quoted in Peter Howell, "Beyoncé Dials It Down," *Toronto Star*, December 12, 2006, D1.

15. Quoted in Elio Iannacci, "Queen B," *Flare*, December 2006, www.findarticles.com (accessed June 6, 2008).

16. Quoted in Valdes.

17. Quoted in Nicola Hodgson, *Beyoncé Knowles* (Chicago: Raintree, 2006), 29.

18. Quoted in "Beyoncé: Bio," www.biggeststars.com (accessed April 18, 2008).

19. Quoted by Emma Johnson, "Diva Wows Crowd," *Manchester Evening News*, November 4, 2003, www.manchesteronline.co.uk (accessed April 16, 2008).

20. Quoted in Simon Garfield, "Uh-Oh! Uh-Oh! Uh-Oh!" *Observer*, December 14, 2003, www.guardian.co.uk (accessed April 16, 2008).

21. Ibid.

22. Quoted by Neil Drumming, "Tour Report: Ladies First," April 2, 2004, www.ew.com (accessed April 16, 2008).

23. Quoted by Eric Myshrall, "Ladies First in Hartford," *The Daily Campus*, April 13, 2004, www.dailycampus.com (accessed April 16, 2008).

24. Quoted by Christina Fuoco, "Live Review: Beyoncé, Alicia Keys and Missy Elliott in Phoenix," April 16, 2004, www.livedaily.com (accessed April 16, 2008).

25. Quoted by Eric Myshrall, "Ladies First in Hartford," *The Daily Campus*, April 13, 2004, www.dailycampus.com (accessed April 16, 2008).

26. Quoted in Rosa Waters, *Hip-Hop: Beyoncé* (Woodall, PA: Mason Crest Publishers, 2007), 40.

27. Quoted by Kelefa Sanneh, "New CD's: Destiny's Child 'Destiny Fulfilled,'" *New York Times*, Nov. 22, 2004, www.nytimes.com (accessed April 26, 2008).

28. Quoted by Associated Press, "Trio Regroups After Beyoncé's Breakout Year, But For How Long?" *News-Star*, Nov. 24, 2004, www.news-star.com (accessed April 16, 2008).

29. Quoted in Denise Sheppard, "Destiny's Take a Bow," *Rolling Stone*, September 12, 2005, www.find.galegroup.com (accessed April 16, 2008).

Chapter 6

BUSY IN BUSINESS

By 2006, only 10 years after Beyoncé and Destiny's Child signed their first recording contract, Beyoncé had become a wealthy woman. Much of the credit goes to her parents, who from the start were determined to operate a family-controlled enterprise because the evidence indicated that other cultures owning businesses that employed family members, such as the Chinese or Koreans, maximized their profits. So the Beyoncé Enterprise prospered with the assistance of Tina, who designed Destiny's Child's costumes and still consults on Beyoncé's wardrobes; Mathew, who conducted Destiny's Child's business matters and still repeats that role with Beyoncé; and Beyoncé's first cousin, Angela Beyence, Beyoncé's personal assistant. Off and on Solange performed on Beyoncé's tours, and she also consults for the Knowles fashion line, House of Dereon.

DIVISION OF LABOR

As financial steward of Destiny's Child/Beyoncé, Mathew safeguarded his child's financial future because this fell under the heading of good parenting. Tina and Mathew monitored expenditures so the girls would have enough put aside for the future. The Knowles also divided the burden of responsibility for parenting and supervising Beyoncé, as well as developing her talent. While Mathew booked performances and haggled over contracts with recording executives, Tina watched out for the girls' health, safety, and well-being. She and Mathew knew the importance of maintaining Destiny's Child's image and not caving in to corporate pressures. So it made sense for Tina to take on the role of stylist on and off stage since the decision would lower overhead and at the same time allow Tina to indulge her creativity while catering to each girl's individual body proportions and personality. Designing and sewing the costumes alone took Tina hours because Mathew insisted on new wardrobes for each promotional appearance, and Tina also styled each girl's hair.

SERVICE PROVIDER

Tina's indispensable services as a costume, fashion, and hair stylist for Destiny's Child were only a warm up for Act Two: couturier. In 2004, Tina combined couturier with entrepreneur and created the House of Dereon clothing line. Regularly commuting from Houston to New York, she operates a hands-on business with duties that include sketching ideas, choosing fabrics, and fitting clothes. Since the House of Dereon debuted, Tina has expanded her line, going beyond junior and women's sportswear to handbags, shoes, and accessories; outerwear; hats; leg wear; and intimate apparel. House of Dereon fashions are on the racks of higher-end department stores and can be purchased online at shop.com, where it competes with brands such as Baby Phat, JLo by Jennifer Lopez, Calvin Klein, and DKNY.

House of Dereon has not always run smoothly; legal problems accompanied its growth, as in July 2006, when Greg Walker, CEO of Icon Entertainment, filed a breach of contract suit against Beyoncé and Tina in New York's Supreme Court. Hired to help secure endorsement licensing deals, Walker negotiated a $15 million agreement with clothing manufacturer Wear Me Apparel and claimed he collected only $25,000 in commissions, significantly less than the amount agreed on. In March 2007, Justice Herman Cahn tossed out the breach-of-contract case because there was no written contract and according to Cahn, Walker, who received a total of $110,000 from the Wear Me Apparel deal, would not receive further money.[1]

SHOW ME THE MONEY

Before managing Destiny's Child, Beyoncé's father, a sales dynamo from day 1, sold medical equipment for Xerox, a position that earned him a six-figure salary. Today, Mathew is widely regarded as a mover and shaker in the pop and R&B music industry, because, as president and CEO of Music World Entertainment, he and his company label—Music World Music—sold more than 200 million records as of 2008.[2] This included CD releases by Sunshine Anderson, Chaka Kahn, The O'Jays, and, of course,

Beyoncé, Solange, and Destiny's Child. Mathew also heads up Music World Properties, an investment company dealing with commercial and residential real estate.

Mathew's successes derive from a commonsense philosophy that says good salespersons can transfer their skills and excel in any industry. At the start of his music career, he felt more qualified than 75 percent of managers because of his knowledge of corporate culture, politics, and the common traits of successful people such as a passion for their work, an ability to think outside of the box, and the willingness to put in extra effort to make a good project great.

To maximize his sales skills in the music industry, Mathew enrolled in the course, Survey of the Music Business, at Houston Community College, which was taught by Aubrey Tucker, a seasoned trombonist who played with some of the best instrumentalists in the industry. The course provided an overview of the recording business, including such functions as artist and repertoire (A&R), promotion, marketing, and business affairs. Tucker's breadth of knowledge was wide; he was a composer, arranger, conductor, and band leader and played classical as well as pop music. He also accompanied stars like Elvis, Frank Sinatra, Natalie Cole, and Tony Bennett. Mathew soaked up class lectures and discussions "like a sponge,"[3] then put everything to work marketing Destiny's Child and, later, daughter Beyoncé as commodities. Through Music World Entertainment, Mathew lived his Motown dream of handling artistic development—from boot camp, vocal lessons, and stage presence to glamour, media training, and debut—and sold the label in 2003 to Sanctuary for $10 million.[4] Still the head of the urban and gospel division in Houston, Mathew received a Doctor of Humane Letters in May 2008 from his alma mater, Fisk University, in honor of his business achievements.

FOLLOW THE LEADER

With business-savvy parents like Tina and Mathew, it was inevitable that Beyoncé would hop on the capitalistic band wagon by negotiating endorsement contracts and hawking fashions under the House of Dereon label. In January 2008, *Forbes Magazine* placed Beyoncé on its Cash Queens list with other divas (such as Barbra Streisand, Celine Dion, and Faith Hill), calling her the "endorsement darling" because of her seven-figure contracts with L'Oreal, American Express, and Samsung.[5] Actually, multiple endorsement deals are not uncommon for today's well-known musical artists, according to James McQuivey, author of *The End of the Music Industry as We Know It*, since the days when an artist such as

Michael Jackson struck one high-profile deal with a corporate giant such as Pepsi have ended.[6] Artists now use their music as promotional tools to market their brands of clothes, perfumes, and other consumer products. Artists promote themselves more today because big record companies do less of it. Some songwriters also license their music to corporations who advertise on television and radio, and it's doubtful that many artists' careers today are compromised by overexposure in commercials.

THE NAME GAME

Beyoncé first waded into product endorsement in 1999 when Pro-Line Corporation, based in Houston, Texas, approached Destiny's Child and asked the group to promote Pro-Line's botanical hair products during an upcoming concert tour after the release of Destiny's Child's second album, *The Writing's on the Wall*. The four young women agreed to appear live in 10 markets nationwide and, depending on the venue—salon, retail, or commercial—the Pro-Line campaign used various promotional packages including life-size displays of Destiny's Child, samples of hair products, entry forms, a participation packet, and CDs. Seated next to a contest sign-up area for 18- to-25-year-old women, Beyoncé and the other girls autographed items while consumers entered a contest for a year's worth of hairstyling from the winner's favorite salon. While on tour in July 2001, Destiny's Child performed at the Essence Music Festival in New Orleans, an event sponsored by Pro-Line and other name companies.

Candie's Shoes

In 2000, Destiny's Child negotiated a second endorsement package with New York-based Candie's shoes, and the group agreed to perform a live concert for customers, participate in a LIVE online chat, and make two in-store appearances. Candie's wanted Destiny's Child because the company considered Beyoncé and the other young women the hottest girl group in music history and recognizable fashion figures. For its part, Candie's gave away hundreds of free tickets to Destiny's Child's 2001 tour and ran a contest for a free trip for the taping of the group's next music video.

Destiny's Dolls

In 2001, Beyoncé, Michelle, and Kelly signed a contract with Hasbro to produce 12-inch dolls in their images. The dolls, which were dressed in costumes identical to those the trio wore at the 2001 Grammy Awards Show, sold for $12.99 in stores and Beyoncé was thrilled that little girls would enjoy them. Then in 2005, despite Destiny's Child's breakup, Mattel marketed Barbie-style look-alike dolls that retailed for $20 each and modeled copies of dresses Destiny's Child wore at the 2004 Fashion Rocks Concert in New York. Hasbro no longer makes the dolls, but they can be purchased as collectibles on E-Bay and other similar venues. Starting in 2006, Mattel unveiled star "bratz" dolls (Beyoncé, Paris Hilton, Lindsay Lohan, etc.), which stand 12 inches tall. Children control the dolls' facial expressions—smiling, pouting, smirking, and so on—by manipulating controls on the doll's back—an advantage that allows consumers more freedom of expression.

Pepsi

In 2002, Beyoncé signed with Pepsi to appear in at least two TV commercials created by director Spike Lee. She also agreed to star in radio and Internet ads as well as a Pepsi-sponsored tour, as "Beyoncé's popularity resonates with a remarkably broad audience," said Randy Melville, then vice president of multiculturalism for Pepsi.[7] Starring in a one-day ad with Britney Spears and Pink, Beyoncé received $3.5 million,[8] but several years later, Pepsi dropped Beyoncé, citing too-much celebrity recognition as the reason—the result of the brand eclipsing the product. Advertising campaigns using Beyoncé's name normally succeed when they pitch products linked to the particularly lucrative teenage market, because adolescents influence adults to purchase items for them or spend their own funds (Harris Interactive, a market research firm, estimates that 8- to 21-year-olds in America have $211 billion in disposable income).[9]

Eau De Beyoncé

In January 2004, Beyoncé teamed up with clothes designer Tommy Hilfiger and endorsed his perfume, True Gold. Hilfiger chose Beyoncé because she epitomized today's woman—sophisticated, beautiful, and talented—and True Star, which combined flowers with grains and aimed for warmth and femininity. The perfume debuted in June 2004 before a global press party in London, and the ad campaign featured Beyoncé singing "Wishing on a Star" a cappella in a video commercial. Beyoncé said her goal was to form a "signature-like" association in the public's mind between the fragrance and herself,[10] and her endorsement increased Beyoncé's bank account by about $3 million.[11]

In 2007, Beyoncé again marketed a fragrance, this time in an expensively choreographed black-and-white video distributed globally in which she danced and sang to the tune, "Diamonds Are a Girl's Best Friend." The scent was "Diamonds," the company Giorgio Armani, and Beyoncé appeared in print and TV ads, jumpstarting the European campaign in Milan. When she launched the U.S. campaign at the Herald Square Macy's in New York City, she personally distributed perfume to the first 150 people.

L'Oreal

In 2004, Beyoncé signed a $4.7 million, five-year deal with L'Oreal[12] in which the contract stipulated it would pay $25,000 a day for two extra 10-hour "service days"[13] and Beyoncé would pose for photo shoots 10 days a year, make promotional and personal appearances, keep her hair in excellent condition, and notify the company if she planned on any radical changes to her hairdo. Beyoncé is also prohibited from buying toiletries at bargain superstores (since her face appears on store advertisements) and cannot use Revlon or Clairol products. In 2007, L'Oreal helped sponsor *The Beyoncé Experience* tour.

DirecTV

In 2007, Beyoncé appeared in a gold form-fitting dress on a DirecTV video that aimed to get customers to upgrade DirecTV to High Definition. Surrounded by male dancers, Beyoncé, using a sexy voice, delivered the message, "Let me upgrade you to the best channels in HD."[14] She also appeared on the December 2007 cover and inside pages of *Access DirecTV*, DirecTV's subscriber magazine, touting the cable company's 100 HD-channel lineup, ranking it Number 1 among its competitors and plugging Control Room, a digital network on DirecTV that airs live entertainment from artists such as Beyoncé, Rod Stewart, and the Rolling Stones.

Samsung Phone

In 2007, Beyoncé and Samsung collaborated on a project to hawk the company's mobile phone, which was designed for active music fans and embedded with Beyoncé's hit single "Irreplaceable" (from her *B'Day* album). She appeared in TV commercials, print ads, global concert tours, and other promotional activities. Later that year Samsung advertised the B' Phone, a special limited-edition phone preloaded with a Beyoncé start-up screen, available through Sprint and with content that included photos, video, and a song sung by Beyoncé at age 10.

Disney

In 2007, Beyoncé set a new high for the number of product endorsements, when she contracted to appear as Alice in Wonderland in a Disneyland ad photographed by renowned photographer Annie Liebovitz. Liebovitz shot images of Beyoncé and other celebrities for publication in the March 2007 issues of *Vogue, Vanity Fair, W, GQ, Conde Nast Traveller, Cookie,* and *The New Yorker.* Liebovitz suggested Beyoncé for "Alice," and Beyoncé agreed because Liebovitz impressed her as a photographic genius.

"It was freezing cold in the teacup," Beyoncé said," but it didn't matter because we were all so excited and it was shot really fast."[15] The shoot was on Liebovitz's farm in upstate New York, where the Disney Company had shipped several teacups, each weighing several hundred pounds and positioned into place by a forklift. Beyoncé earned an undisclosed amount for her work.

Got Milk?

Beyoncé and Tina participated in the dairy industry's "Got Milk?" campaign, which encouraged people to drink milk to stay slim. The ad emphasized how role modeling by moms can establish healthy eating/drinking habits in daughters and grandchildren. Because the Hispanic market for milk (and other commodities) has expanded to 43 million people (the current disposable income for Hispanics is $863 billion, according to a study by the Selig Center for Economic Growth at the University of Georgia),[16] Beyoncé was warned against literal Spanish translations of sound bites; for instance, "Got milk?" in Spanish translates as "Are you lactating?" which would be an embarrassing, if not financially irresponsible, mistake!

American Express

In September 2007, American Express closed a multimillion-dollar endorsement deal with Beyoncé based, in part, on her crossover ethnic appeal (like Tiger Woods). Celebrated photographer Annie Liebovitz again photographed Beyoncé for the print campaign while a television video directed by Paul Hunter was filmed in New York in August 2007. The video showed Beyoncé's average day—a hectic schedule of family visits and shopping excursions sandwiched in between press conferences, photo shoots, and dance rehearsals. Beyoncé's parents and assorted family members appeared in cameos, and the video focused on Beyoncé relaxing in her hotel room after shopping online with her American Express Card.

House of Dereon

The goal behind the House of Dereon (named after Beyoncé's grandmother, Agnes Dereon, a seamstress) is to transform the mediocre into the marvelous, according to press release hype, which also maintains that Tina supplies the couture, Beyoncé the kick, and Agnes Dereon the soul. Beyoncé and her former partner Kelly model for the company. "I was adamant about not putting my name on something that I didn't love," said Beyoncé. "I wanted to make sure it was true and honest and really something that we designed."[17] In 2007, Beyoncé appeared topless in an ad for House of Dereon jeans, and the line later unveiled clothes for infants, children, and larger size women. (The "Miss Tina" label is marketed on the Home Shopping Network.)

Thanks to Tina's lengthy experience coordinating Destiny's Child's costumes and tailoring hot pants, cropped tops, black leather pants, and mix-and-match crystal-studded bras for Beyoncé and her colleagues, Tina felt at home in a couturier setting. The House of Dereon, which debuted on "Oprah" and was featured on *The Tyra Banks Show*, offered ready-to-wear clothes and accessories retailing from $100 to $500. But not everyone thinks so highly of the Dereon line. One critic said Tina dressed Beyoncé like a middle-age woman; another said Tina outfitted her at The Fashion Rocks show like a matador. Reporter Robin Givhan wrote that Destiny's Child always looked like Vegas bridesmaids.[18]

In early 2008, and with slipping sales, Beyoncé and Tina devised a mobile game with online social networking. In Beyoncé Fashion Diva, players create their own unique diva, using clothes from the Dereon line. They also can mix and match hairstyles and facial features and connect and share with other game players online. As a child, Beyoncé loved to play dress up, which is what Fashion Diva allows players to do. It is available through Samsung's B'Phone; accompanying MP3 players also air clips of Beyoncé's hit songs.

Although the company did not become an instant success, it repositioned itself as a line of evening wear (gowns range from $300 to $500), and a majority of sales come from its junior sportswear. In August 2008, *Newsweek Magazine* said despite House of Dereon's ample media exposure, it failed to resonate with consumers.[19] In October 2008, however, Beyoncé and Tina promoted the new House of Dereon dress collection based on the movie "Cadillac Records" at Bloomingdale's, New York.

MY MONEY'S ON YOU

The bottom line in business is money, and Beyoncé has produced extremely healthy numbers. According to Rob LaFranco, a former editor for *Forbes* and compiler of "Rock's Top 30 Moneymakers" (*Rolling Stone*), Destiny's Child scored Number 14 on the 2006 list.[20] The all-time most popular girl group netted $24.8 million after paying off managers, agents, and other members of their entourage.[21]

In 2008, *Forbes Magazine* listed the 10 top-earning African American celebrities, and Beyoncé's $27 million put her at Number 9.[22] *Forbes* attributed her wealth to endorsements with blue chip brands like American Express and the album, *B'Day*, which sold more than 7 million copies worldwide (enormous record sales usually lead to enormous concert sales, but since Beyoncé prefers to keep concert figures private, it is unknown how her *Beyoncé Experience* tour fared financially. "I don't think it's anyone's business," she said[23]). That said, in September 2008, BET Entertainment announced that from June 2007 to June 2008, Beyoncé raked in $80 million, making her music's second-highest-paid entertainer. She also sold $50 million in tickets on her last tour and released a new album in November 2008.

THE "M" WORD

Whether or not Beyoncé and Jay-Z intend their marriage to be a merger or not, the extraordinary wealth on both sides adds another dimension to their alliance. Although a prenuptial agreement safeguards each person's individual assets, any money or properties gained after April 3, 2008 (this includes the 15,000-square-foot modern colonial the couple recently purchased in Scarsdale and any profits currently derived from businesses or companies Beyoncé or Jay-Z establishes individually or together) are considered joint property in New York State (the couple was married in Scarsdale, New York). Beyoncé and Jay-Z cannot touch each other's "separate property" (assets owned before the marriage or property acquired through an inheritance or gift).

Vibe reported much of the terms of the prenuptial contract, which indicates if the marriage ends within two years, Jay-Z will pay Beyoncé $10 million. Jay-Z also pledged to give Beyoncé $1 million for each year she stayed married to him—up to 15 years. The payout could go as high as

$25 million if the two divorce. Beyoncé also gets $5 million for each child she bears—this compensates for the loss of income during her pregnancy/motherhood.

At the same time as Jay-Z and Beyoncé negotiated the prenuptial agreement, the groom culminated a 15-year deal with Live Nation, which promotes and produces concerts for big-name artists. Jay-Z raked in $150 million and 775,000 shares of Live Nation stock from that transaction.[24]

NOTES

1. "House of Dereon Accused of Racism," April 3, 2007, www.hiphop.popcrunch.com (accessed September 6, 2008).

2. "Music World Entertainment Partners with Essence . . .," June 18, 2008, www.marketwatch.com (accessed September 6, 2008).

3. Quoted by Mary Dawson, *How to Get Somewhere in the Music Business* (Dallas, TX: CQK Books, 2007), 183.

4. "Beyoncé's Dad Sells Music Company for $10 Million," *Jet*, October 27, 2003, www.findarticles.com (accessed September 6, 2008).

5. Quoted by Dorothy Pomerantz, "The Top-Earning Women in Music," *Forbes Magazine*, January 29, 2008, www.find.galegroup.com (accessed April 15, 2008).

6. Charles Moran, "Indie Act Seeks Backup Brand; In Today's World, 'Selling Out' Is the Only Way to Cash In," *Advertising Age*, March 10, 2008, www.find.galegroup.com (accessed April 15, 2008).

7. Quoted by Stephen M. Silverman, "Beyoncé Bounces Britney from Pepsi Ads," *People*, December 18, 2002, www.people.com (accessed April 15, 2008).

8. "Britney, Beyoncé, Pink—We Will Rock You," www.celeb-update.com (accessed September 6, 2008).

9. "Generation Y Earns $211 Billion," *Harris Interactive*, 2003, www.emeraldinsight.com (accessed September 6, 2008).

10. Quoted in "Tommy Hilfiger and Beyoncé Unveil True Star," *Press Release*, June 21, 2004, www.tommy.com (accessed April 15, 2008).

11. Steve Hall, "Beyoncé Signs Deal with Hilfiger to Boost Fragrance," January 27, 2004, www.adrants.com (accessed September 6, 2008).

12. Apryl Duncan, "Beyoncé Signs Endorsement Deal with L'Oreal," August 30, 2004, www.advertising.about.com (accessed September 6, 2008).

13. "Cosmetics Deals Ruin Beyoncé Knowles' Shopping Hobby," *The Hindustan Times*, September 18, 2006, www.hindustantimes.com (accessed April 15, 2008).

14. Todd Spangler, "Fitting on the HD Shelf," *Multichannel News*, December 3, 2007, www.highbeam.com (accessed September 10, 2008).

15. Quoted by William Keck, "Disney's Dazzling 'Dreams," *USA Today*, January 25, 2007, www.usatoday.com (accessed April 15, 2008).

16. Jerry Large, "Seattle Times Jerry Large Column: Marketing Target: Hispanics," *Seattle Times*, April 12, 2007, www.newsbank.com (accessed April 15, 2008).

17. Quoted in "The Beyoncé Experience," *Cosmopolitan*, www.cosmopolitan.com (accessed April 15, 2008).

18. Quoted by Robin Givhan, "Destiny's Child, Sequin New Horizons," *Washington Post*, June 17, 2005. C1.

19. "Newsweek Magazine: Beyoncé's House of Dereon Clothing Line Is a Failure," August 12, 2008, www.mediatakeout.com (accessed November 1, 2008).

20. Rob La Franco, "Rock's Top 30 Money Makers" in "The Richest Rock Stars of 2006" by Brian Hiatt, *Rolling Stone*, March 10, 2006, www.ebscohost.com (accessed April 15, 2008).

21. Ibid

22. Lea Goldman, "The Top-Earning African-American Stars," *Forbes*, February 4, 2008, www.ebscohost.com (accessed April 15, 2008).

23. Quoted by Lisa Robinson, "Beyoncé," *Vanity Fair*, November 2005, www.find.galegroup.com (accessed April 15, 2008).

24. Glenn Gamboa, "Jay-Z, Live Nation Strike $150 Million Deal," April 13, 2008, www.newsday.com (accessed September 6, 2008).

Chapter 7

PHILANTHROPY

Giving back to the greater community is not only part of the Judeo-Christian and Western traditions. Many believe it is a moral responsibility that individuals usually fulfill through volunteerism and/or philanthropy. Local scout and service organizations and regional or national nonprofits regularly solicit unpaid workers to perform valuable humanitarian duties, and many people donate money, clothing, cars, and other tangibles for purchase, auction, or raffling at local fundraisers. Wealthy business people and celebrities such as Bill Gates, Warren Buffett, and Oprah often set up deep-pocket trusts for worthwhile causes. For many of the rich and famous whose earnings have reached startling new heights, philanthropy is an acquired taste. With increased income and visibility come greater pressures and expectations. Average citizens and government agencies look to the private sector for endowments and trusts to finance research for new vaccines and other cures, to support the arts, and to supplement other government resources. In an effort to be good role models and exemplify benevolence and selflessness, celebrities often act as spokespersons for causes: Mary Tyler Moore for juvenile diabetes, Elizabeth Taylor for AIDS, and Marlo Thomas for St. Jude Children's Hospital.

Through appeals to the ego, guilt, and a grab basket of mixed emotions, celebrities often are motivated to give of themselves and their wealth. Guilt and good intentions are not the only reasons high-profile personalities support health, environmental, and other causes; another factor is image. Publicists know that clients who position themselves to receive positive media attention enhance their images and further their careers. This is not to imply that every sports personality or Las Vegas magician waging war against the disease or the disaster of the month devotes himself or herself to a cause only because it may prove lucrative; but entertainers who donate time, energy, and/or cash to community service and national efforts almost always get back much more than they give either monetarily or in more intangible ways.

BENEFIT CONCERTS

Beyoncé's introduction to fundraising started with two benefit concerts for the victims of 9/11. On October 20, 2001, Destiny's Child, among other well-known artists, performed at Madison Square Garden in New York City and more than $30 million[1] was collected. The money went to the Robin Hood Relief and Twin Towers Funds, both established by Mayor Rudolph Giuliani to benefit rescue workers. The VH1 concert, at which Destiny's Child sang "Emotions" and "The Gospel Medley," presented a star-studded lineup of actors, musicians, and vocal groups that included Billy Joel, David Spade, Susan Sarandon, Paul McCartney, Elton John, and Bon Jovi.

The next day Destiny's Child appeared at an hours-long ABC-televised concert at RFK Stadium in Washington, D.C., organized by pop music icon Michael Jackson and hosted by John Stamos and Kevin Spacey. Washington, D.C. politicians spoke, and guests such as Carole King, James Brown, The Backstreet Boys, Pink, and Rod Stewart entertained a live audience during which time Destiny's Child sang the song "Survivor." Additional money was also raised from album collaboration between Destiny's Child, Justin Timberlake, Alicia Keys, Usher, and Gwen Stefani; portions of the proceeds from the single *What's Going On* were funneled to the United Way's September 11th Fund and the AIDS relief effort.

MANDELA'S AIDS SHOW

In 2003, the AIDS cause again motivated Beyoncé and Bono to head an international charity show sponsored by the Nelson Mandela Foundation to which Beyoncé donated a percentage of the gross receipts from her *Dangerously in Love* tour. The benefit took place at the Greenpoint Stadium in Cape Town, South Africa, and acts included the Eurythmics, Yvonne Chaka, and Peter Gabriel. Besides raising money for AIDS research, the concert's goal was to further an awareness of the disease for a global television, radio, and online audience of about 2 billion people.[2] Donations poured in from tracks downloaded off the Internet and from combined DVD and CD concert sales. Beyoncé and Bono performed the duet "American Prayer," which described the churches that opened their doors to AIDS victims and helped to eradicate the stigma of HIV. The audience heard that the number of AIDS deaths was more than the number of casualties from all the wars, famines, and floods throughout history; and the audience also heard recorded messages from former President Clinton, Robert DeNiro, Sir Ian McKellen, and singer Annie Lennox.

CANCER BENEFIT

In April 2004, Beyoncé and other celebrities such as Glenn Close, Whoopi Goldberg, Carly Simon, and Nathan Lane entertained at a charity gala aboard the Queen Mary 2 in New York City. The theme was "Hollywood Hits Broadway," and the benefit, which Katie Couric and the Entertainment Industry Foundation sponsored to honor Couric's late husband, Jay Monahan—a victim of colon cancer—poured money into the National Colorectal Cancer Research Alliance. A few years later, on September 5, 2008, Beyoncé appeared with 14 other female singers, including Melissa Etheridge, Fergie, and Sheryl Crow, to perform the song "Just Stand Up" to raise money for cancer research. The song was aired as part of a one-hour, star-studded fundraiser, "Stand Up to Cancer," simultaneously broadcast on three networks and seen in 170-plus countries. More than $100 million was raised, and all proceeds from sales of the record went to cancer research.[3]

DIABETES BENEFIT

In 2004, Beyoncé donated her talents to an invitation-only Beverly Hills soiree for juvenile diabetes attended by people from movie studios, television networks, talent agencies, and the music industry. The guest list included stars like Natalie Cole, Ray Romano, Forest Whitaker, and Muhammad Ali, with such featured performers as Faith Hill and Josh Groban. A silent auction highlighted the program, with donated prizes that ranged from jewelry, haute couture, and luxury vacations to celebrity-painted china and designer-decorated pedal cars from Mercedes Benz.

SAVE THE MUSIC

In June 2005, Beyoncé hosted a reception/auction at the Museum of Television and Radio in New York on behalf of the VH1 Save the Music Foundation. With her mother alongside, the glamorous singer exhibited 18 to 24 of her sexiest, most memorable dresses and costumes (outfits included ones designed for the 2004 Grammys and the *Dangerously in Love* album), then kicked off the bidding on them. Although Beyoncé senti-mentalized selling the gowns, she felt the money raised was for an impor-tant cause: to further music education programs for public schoolchildren across the country.

WORLD CHILDREN'S DAY

McDonald's World Children's Day, observed globally on November 20, raises money for the Ronald McDonald Houses, Family Rooms, Care Mo-bile programs, and other resources for ill children. The World Children's Day anthem, "Stand Up for Love," was written by Beyoncé and David Foster to honor and highlight the contributions of volunteers and pro-fessionals who help sick children. Destiny's Child was appointed global ambassador for 2005 and through McDonald's network and its World Children's Day, more than $440 million in grants and programs were al-located to sick children.[4] Beyoncé met many of the beneficiaries of those programs during her *Destiny Fulfilled* and *Lovin' It* tours and Destiny's Child, which received the Caring Hands, Caring Hearts Award from Mc-Donald's in appreciation of its role as global ambassadors, donated an ad-ditional 25 cents from every ticket purchased for their North American tour to Ronald McDonald House Charities.

FASHION FOR RELIEF

On September 16, 2005, Beyoncé and other celebrities pitched in to help Hurricane Katrina victims by participating in the Fashion for Relief benefit, which was held in Bryant Park in Manhattan. Organized by su-permodel Naomi Campbell and narrated by Sarah Ferguson, the event attracted more than 1,000 people, with proceeds going to AmeriCares.[5] Runway fashions, which Beyoncé modeled, as did Nichole Richie, Wyclef Jean, Sean "Diddy" Combs, Rachel Hunter, Kelly Osbourne, Amerie, and other stars, were auctioned off a few days later on the Internet at Yahoo.com.

FORUM AGAINST VIOLENCE

In August 2007, Beyoncé took a break from raising money to raise spir-its. She spoke to about seventy 12- to 18-year-old girls at a Defining Our Own Destiny forum in Washington, D.C., an event organized by District Council member Kwame R. Brown, who recognized that the D.C. area lacked an antiviolence program for girls.[6] Brown convinced organizations such as Covenant House Washington, Peaceoholics/C.H.O.I.C.E., and the Mayor's Youth Leadership Institute to sponsor a special forum with the goal of ending violence in many of the district's embattled neighborhoods and spreading the message that you can overcome challenges. Brown chose Beyoncé because of her national recognition as a good role model, and the forum offered discussions on reaching goals despite obstacles, keeping a healthy self-image, and endeavoring to act as a community peacemaker.

HELPING HURRICANE VICTIMS

In December 2002, Destiny's Child dedicated the new $1.2-million youth center adjacent to St. John's United Methodist Church in downtown Houston, where Beyoncé still attends services.[7] The Knowles family and Kelly donated $500,000 to the construction of the center, which hosts many activities (including scouts, sex education classes, mentoring, career development and tutoring programs, and summer camp) and supports a basketball court, a recording studio, a risk reduction program called Breaking the Silence, and a youth HIV education program. Beyoncé hoped the center—a substitute for the supportive environments found lacking in many children's homes—would encourage kids to have fun and learn things to help them resist the negative outlets and influences in their lives.

THE SURVIVOR FOUNDATION

After Hurricane Katrina in 2005, Beyoncé, her parents, and Kelly founded the Houston-based Survivor Foundation, a nonprofit group that assisted hurricane victims, paying for 160 students from the charter school, Houston Can! Academy, to view the movie *Freedom Riders* and for 50 music students from Beverly Hills Intermediate School in Houston to attend the Midwest Clinic International Band and Orchestra Conference—one of the nation's most esteemed events.[8] Other money raised from a Christmas carnival held in cooperation with Music World Entertainment for 300 low-income households went to House of Dereon clothes for one hurricane survivor and for the Survivor Starter Kit, which provided six months of supplemental housing, job training/placement, and transportation to displaced individuals and families and former offenders. Furthermore, a plan to supply long-term transitional housing also was conceived, and on September 12, 2007, a groundbreaking ceremony took place in downtown Houston for the Knowles-Rowland Temenos Place Apartments. When constructed, this facility will be a 43-residence, single-room-occupancy project cosupported by the Foundation and St. John's United Methodist Church.

In October 2008, after the devastation wrought by Hurricane Ike to the Greater Houston area, Beyoncé donated $100,000 to the Gulf Coast Ike Relief Fund. The Survivor Foundation and the Knowles family donated the use of the House of Dereon Media Center in Houston to an engaged couple in need of a venue for their wedding. The Survivor Foundation also urged other companies (caterers, limousine, videographer, wedding coordinator, makeup) to donate their services for the wedding.

GLOBAL FOOD DRIVE

During *The Beyoncé Experience* tour in 2007, Beyoncé held food drives in different cities in North America, partnering with Pastor Rudy Rasmus of St. John's United Methodist Church in Houston and using her tour to encourage fans to donate nonperishable food items in exchange for autographed photos of the super star. Her goals were to have her fans enjoy the empowering experience of making a difference and to help the Global FoodBanking Network, America's Second Harvest, and The Nation's Food Bank Network, organizations that regularly feed hungry people in the United States and in heavily populated countries such as Ethiopia, Turkey, and India.

Mathew and Tina also share credit for the food drive, and this global contribution was recognized recently by the PTA, the national parent-teacher association. In October 2008, the Knowles received the esteemed National PTA Commitment to America's Children Award at a formal gala in Chicago, Illinois. The tribute acknowledged the couple's contributions in establishing Houston's Knowles-Rowland Center for Youth, the Survivor Foundation, and the Knowles-Rowland Temenos Place Apartments in Houston.

ROBIN HOOD

In 2006, Beyoncé and other celebrities performed at a New York City charter school fundraiser supported by the Robin Hood Foundation, an organization that pioneered what *Fortune Magazine* called venture philanthropy (in this case, for example, the school board members paid the nonprofit's administrative costs, so all money raised went to the cause). The gala brought in $48 million to fight poverty in New York, and among the auctioned prizes were 10 power lunch dates with celebrities like the CEOs of J. P. Morgan, Chase, Viacom, and Time; lessons with surfer Kelly Slater; a ride on Jimmy Buffett's sea plane to the Hamptons or Martha's Vineyard; and an evening for 500 people at Six Flags Great Adventure Park.[9] The fundraiser also raised $1 million from naming rights, with 30 classroom names earning a total of $250,000 (one of the rooms was named for Jay-Z of Def Jam Recordings).[10]

PRINCE'S TRUST URBAN MUSIC FESTIVAL

In May 2004, Jay-Z and Beyoncé and other renowned artists like Alicia Keys, The Streets, and Amy Winehouse performed in London for the Prince's Trust at Earl's Court, where about 30,000 fans assembled. The Prince's Trust, which was founded by Prince Charles in 1976, endeavors to help young people fulfill their potential by means of training, mentoring, and financial assistance. The IRC (Information Relay Center) has helped more than 500,000 14- to 30-year-olds.[11] A dress rehearsal for the festival, after which Beyoncé and Jay-Z attended a dinner hosted by Prince Charles at Buckingham Palace, took place at the University of Westminster campus in northwest London, where live radio shows were broadcast from backstage.

HIP-HOP SUMMIT

In January 2004, Beyoncé hosted Houston's Hip-Hop Summit, which was sponsored by the Hip-Hop Summit Action Network—a national organization of artists and entrepreneurs and the brainchild of hip-hop pioneer Russell Simmons and Dr. Benjamin Chavis, the former executive director of the National African-American Leadership Summit and the organizer of the Million Man Marches. More than 20,000 newly registered voters attended the event, which helps black youths learn empowerment strategies.[12] Beyoncé, Mathew, and Solange participated in the Network's 2007 National Financial Empowerment Tour, which instructed young people in banking, repairing and understanding credit scores, asset and wealth management, vehicle financing, and home ownership (one lecture titled "Get Your Money Right" provided financial basics). In March 2007, the Network presented the Knowles family and Music World Entertainment with the Global Achievement Award for Economic Empowerment for their contributions to the careers of artists such as Destiny's Child, Beyoncé, and Michelle Williams.

TEXAS MUSIC PROJECT

The Texas Music Project (TMP), a statewide program coordinated by Honorary Chairperson Beyoncé, raises money for school music education classes through the sale of *Don't Mess with Texas Music* CDs on which are found Beyoncé's "Dangerously in Love 2" and contributions from other name musicians like Clint Black, Eric Clapton, and Bonnie Raitt. The project's goal is to change children's lives through music, and in 2004 the project distributed $200,000 in grants to Texas schools for music programs.[13]

REEBOK

In 2004, Beyoncé, along with Tyra Banks, Joy Bryant, Fergie, and Queen Latifah, participated in a community outreach program supported by Jay-Z and Reebok, the popular manufacturer of athletic shoes. They designed their own tennis shoes on an Internet Web site (Beyoncé's shoe was a simple white pattern with pink and gray trim), and the shoes were auctioned off in July 2004 to benefit the Shawn Carter Scholarship Fund, which Jay-Z and his mother founded to assist disadvantaged youth and nontraditional high school students who wish to attend college. Bids for the "designer" shoes started at $100 and top bidders got the designer package: the shoe, a sketch of it, and an autograph from the celebrity.

RAISE YOUR RIGHT HAND RING FOR AFRICA

In 2007, the Diamond Information Center supported three projects that benefit various African communities (the umbrella name was Raise Your Right Hand Ring for Africa campaign). Beyoncé, who visited the project when she was in Africa, wore a spectacular 25-carat gray, yellow, and white diamond ring to the 64th Annual Golden Globe Awards red carpet and contributed $10,000 to Link-A-Child, a nonprofit organization that cares for more than 7 million orphaned children and babies in Nigeria.[14]

PHOENIX HOUSE

In 2008 while researching drug addiction and rehabilitation for the movie, *Cadillac Records,* in which Beyoncé portrays heroin addict Etta James, the recording star visited Brooklyn, New York's, Phoenix House, where James was treated in the 1960s. Beyoncé observed hard-core junkies for two weeks and came away extremely moved by the experience. At the time, Beyoncé promised the facility's director, Darnell Martin, that she intended to donate her movie fee to the center. In January 2009 Beyoncé, true to her word, handed over $4 million to the Phoenix House chain.[15]

NOTES

1. "The Concert for New York," www.everything2.com (accessed May 8, 2008).

2. "Beyoncé and Bono Lead AIDS Show," BBC, November 29, 2003, www.bbc.com (accessed May 8, 2008).

3. "News," September 2008, www.standup2cancer.org (accessed September 11, 2008).

4. Ellis Michon, "World Children's Day at McDonald's," November 16, 2006, www.mcdonalds.com (accessed May 8, 2008).

5. "Fashion for Relief," www.hamptons.com (accessed May 8, 2008).

6. "Beyoncé Chats with DC Girls Before Show," August 10, 2007, www.foreverBeyoncé.com (accessed September 7, 2007).

7. "Work Starts on Beyoncé-aided Survivor-related Complex," September 13, 2007, www.houstonhurricanerecovery.org (accessed May 8, 2008).

8. Ibid.

9. Andy Serwer, "The Legend of Robin Hood," *Fortune*, September 8, 2006, //money.cnn.com (accessed September 7, 2008).

10. Ibid.

11. "Prince Charles Meets U.S. Rap Stars," May 7, 2004, www.news.bbc.co.uk (accessed September 7, 2008).

12. "Record Breaking Houston Hip-Hop Summit," February 3, 2004, www.hsan.org (accessed September 7, 2008).

13. "Beyoncé, Clint Black, Eric Clapton and Bonnie Raitt Join the Texas Music Project . . .," September 15, 2004, www.texasmusicproject.org (accessed May 8, 2008).

14. Lorraine Schwartz, "Beyoncé, Jennifer Lopez and Patricia Flash Their Right Hand . . .," January 25, 2007, www.news.sawf.org (accessed September 7, 2007).

15. Mike Parker, "Beyoncé 4M Gift to Addicts," *Daily Star Sunday*, January 4, 2009, www.dailystar.co.uk (accessed January 17, 2009).

Chapter 8

RELATIONSHIPS

Although Beyoncé's prodigious talents rival or surpass those of many artists, her fame extends beyond creative accomplishments. She also is famous for her entourage—the family members, friends, mentors, lovers, and other people with whom she hangs out at posh restaurants, clubs, exclusive vacation resorts, and ordinary places like that Italian grocery store on the corner of Broadway and 85th and that little anonymous hole-in-the-wall café where she can order a latte and biscotti to go and no one will bat an eyelash. Because Beyoncé mixes in sophisticated social circles as a result of her and husband Jay-Z's combined magnetism, Beyoncé has actually become famous for being famous. Peruse the celebrity columns of almost any national newspaper and you will often see Beyoncé mentioned in conjunction with Gwyneth Paltrow and her husband Chris Martin, Tina Knowles, Solange, Kelly Rowland, Michelle Williams, and, of course, Jay-Z. Gossip mongers sometimes try to stir up excitement by pairing Beyoncé with other male entertainment stars in the fraternity—perhaps Kanye West or Ludacris, for instance.

Beyoncé is not the first celebrity to have the "famous for being famous" distinction—the Gabor sisters (Hungarian-born glamour gals Eva, Zsa Zsa, and Magda, who appeared on television in the 1950s and 1960s) invented it; now the Hilton sisters (Paris and Nicky) carry on the grand tradition. Call it the snowball effect or celebrity momentum, but at some point, fame feeds on itself and stars gain more and more power and influence until fans catch themselves wanting flying lessons or planning a vacation at Lake Como because such and such celebrity enthused about it on a late-night talk show. Celebrity influence extends far and wide—notice how the environmental and green movements progressed to the mainstream when stars like *Seinfeld*'s Julia Louis Dreyfus and *Cheers*' Ted Danson began supporting ecological and conservation causes and then onetime vice presidential candidate Al Gore wrote a best seller on global warming.

In a similar manner, Beyoncé has spread a layer of acceptability over close, tightly knit family relationships. By demonstrating the affection and love she feels toward her parents, sister, and close friends Michelle Williams and Kelly Rowland, and by marrying the one man she dated for six years, Beyoncé has made intimacy, and now monogamy and fidelity, trendy again. It is now a force from which many average people worldwide draw the requisite energy to maintain an inner circle of close friends and family.

MAMA MIA

Beyoncé and her mother share a close relationship with occasional flare-ups, but even so, when Beyoncé is on tour and everybody demands so much from her, she is glad to have her mother around. "Your mother just wants you happy," Beyoncé said.[1] Family is the adhesive that binds Beyoncé's professional and personal lives together, and she never goes anywhere without the accompaniment of one or two family members—people who love her and tell her the truth. One of those persons is Tina Knowles, whose so-called stage mother status rivals that of Bernadette Peters's portrayal of Mama Rose in the hit musical revival *Gypsy*. Besides presiding over the House of Dereon—the Knowles family's fashion line—Tina is Beyoncé's stylist, confidante, and frequent travel companion, as well as key contributor to the "family project,"[2] which refers to Beyoncé.

The relationship is reciprocal, however, as Beyoncé worships her mother and feels lucky to have her in her life. She considers Tina a phenomenal woman who easily impresses others and serves as a wonderful role model. Beyoncé solicits her mom's advice, especially on important matters, and learns many lessons from her—two of the most significant being that physical beauty means nothing because it fades, and "everything you do in the dark will one day come to light."[3] Beyoncé believes that emulating her mother will not be easy because Tina always was extremely involved in Beyoncé's daily activities. Although an ambitious entrepreneur in her own right, Tina favors happiness and warm relationships over career, which is why she understood Beyoncé's occasional need to put her professional life on the back burners.

Tina communicated many values to Beyoncé (for example, the value of money) mainly through refusals, such as rejecting Beyoncé's request for an expensive pair of shoes or a party. Also, when she and Mathew exerted control over a young Beyoncé's income, public criticism rankled Tina, but it did not dissuade her from what she perceived as her parental duty to set a good example about finances and savings. Beyoncé also learned acceptance because her mother demonstrated this virtue no matter what Beyoncé's mood was—sad, mad, selfish, mistaken, whatever. The superstar credits her success to her mother's support and love because "Nobody in the world had confidence and believed in us like my mom and dad," she said.[4] A recent development that solidified the mother-daughter relationship is Tina's unqualified approval of Beyoncé's husband, Jay-Z, whom Tina regards as smart, polite, and committed to Beyoncé. Beyoncé appreciated Tina's approval for two reasons: validation of her choice and the shared belief that a secure relationship with a man—unlike the transitory nature of fame—grounds a woman.

HER HEART BELONGS TO DADDY

Mathew and Beyoncé relate to each other as parent and child, but that defines only one aspect of their relationship. One interviewer called it "symbiotic" because of the business arrangement. As Beyoncé's manager, Mathew was the person most responsible for deciding on the trajectory of Beyoncé's career. If Mathew made a mistake and Beyoncé the teenager or young adult became angry, she could not easily cut him out of her life—Dad would still be there in the morning at the breakfast table. And when her Destiny's Child partners went out of town, Beyoncé took orders from her father, such as helping Tina prepare outfits, talking to the record label, and writing video treatments and songs. "If anyone got the least amount of good treatment, it was me," Beyoncé said, "because it's my father and I can't say no."[5]

Beyoncé and Mathew disagree from time to time. It was not an easy thing for Beyoncé to work with her father. "We bump heads, we have arguments,"[6] she said. One area of differences was the appropriate extent of exposure for Destiny's Child—Beyoncé wanted to err on the side of less. Because she pulls the veil of privacy over much of her emotional life, outsiders probably will never know how often the two debated this and other issues, except that when she turned 19, Beyoncé started rejecting certain suggestions and quarrels ensued. Still, as late as 2007, she and her father met weekly to discuss business. Mathew never gave her ultimatums; for example, if she wanted to play a "crack head in a movie in Prague," he probably would defer to her, she said.[7] For that and other reasons, she never fired her father and does not retain him as her manager out of obligation. He performs well in that area and she loves him for that and other things.

As Beyoncé matured, Mathew became more and more of a friend. And like a trusted friend, Mathew tells Beyoncé the raw, unvarnished truth, no matter what, even if it relates to her appearance or performances.

That being the case, Mathew exults in playing diverse roles, sometimes rapidly shifting back and forth between them. As Beyoncé's manager and a former award-winning employee at Xerox, he believed in discipline—setting tough but realistic goals—and carried out a strict work ethic that demanded total concentration and focus from himself and the people he supervised. "We show up and we suit up, and we do whatever it takes to get the job done," Mathew said.[8] As conscientious as he is about work duties, Mathew feels that way about his elder daughter. He wanted two things for Beyoncé—happiness and financial freedom—and, thanks to Mathew, she has always experienced both. Even when her parents separated for six months, she knew that her parents loved her and that her father gave up a secure position with a world-renown corporation—a company that furnished him with prestige and a pension—for her. That Mathew would abandon so much for a daughter's shot at possible success in a volatile industry would make any daughter happy. It did not matter to Mathew what dream Beyoncé chose to pursue. If she had told him she wanted to be a doctor, "I would find a way of buying a hospital," he said.[9] His success at negotiating a recording contract between Destiny's Child and Columbia not only strengthened his bond with Beyoncé, but also validated Mathew, bolstering an ego sorely damaged by domestic problems.

If Beyoncé ever doubted her father's commitment to her and her family, she cast that aside when she tacked on a musical tribute to her father at the end of her *Dangerously in Love* album. With the lyrics, "I want my unborn son to be like my daddy, and my husband to be like my daddy," she confessed her strong love for a parent who helped her achieve happiness and a meaningful career.[10] Beyoncé's intense admiration and love for her father (especially during Destiny's Child's breakup) fueled the public's accusation that she was "Daddy's little girl." She denied the epithet then, but seems reconciled to it now, judging from the inclusion of her "Daddy" track. Although she has said that it's more difficult for her father to let go than her mother, Beyoncé may actually be the one who finds it hardest to let go, despite her protestations of independence. According to Rachel Vassel, who included Beyoncé in her book, *Strong Fathers Make "Fearless" Daughters*, strong fathers teach their daughters to be independent, but also rescue or protect them when necessary.[11]

Beyoncé has enumerated the characteristics she loves most about her father and wished to rediscover in a lover, including sincerity, maturity, goal-focused behavior, independence, and the ability to laugh and make others laugh. It's important for her to be with a man who does not control her because he is too busy mapping out his own life. Control appears to be an important issue for Beyoncé in her relationships with men. For one thing, some fans might have suspected that Mathew's dogmatic, take-no-prisoners attitude was the reason for the LaTavia-LeToya split with Destiny's Child. When Beyoncé was asked about the reason for the breakup, she quickly defended her dad, however: "Saying that you are gonna fire the manager, without the team agreeing to that, is not a good thing," she said.[12] She affixed blame squarely on her former partners and when gossip surfaced about Mathew and the suspected sexual harassment of one of the show's dancers, Beyoncé dismissed it, repeating the refrain that Mathew is protective, a great father, and a wonderful manager, but not a controlling despot, as the media would have it.

Her conflict over her father probably stems from his multiple roles, for not too many fathers put their daughters on a low-fat diet and tell them to run three miles before school or jog a mile while singing to increase stamina. And not too many fathers invite their daughter's best friend (and Destiny's Child partner) to live at their house so they can monitor that person's practice time and other activities. Although these actions could be construed as proof positive of a father's dedication to his daughter's dream, they also bear the unmistakable mark of a salesman intent on controlling the variables and readying his products for market. "If there are some issues that need to be addressed, then I'll put them on the table," Mathew said.[13]

SISTERLY DEVOTION

Beyoncé and her sister Solange—also a songwriter and recording artist (Solange released the album *Solo Star* in 2003 and in August 2008 debuted her sophomore project, *Hadley Street Dreams*)—seem to have escaped the downside of sisterhood, which, of course, is sibling rivalry. This could be the result of above-average parenting from the grandparents down, with its fair and consistent discipline and respect for the uniqueness of each child—techniques that Mathew and Tina learned growing up in child-centered homes with good role models who sacrificed much to further their children's emotional growth, education, and career development.

On the other hand, the lack of sibling rivalry also may result from opposite personalities. Solange—despite her similar career choice—carries different life expectations from those of Beyoncé, as seen in 2004 when Solange was known as the "more independent daughter, the oddball kid sister who seems to enjoy doing things on her own."[14] Her family considered Solange a nonconformist in dress and in the kind of music she wrote and produced, in her image, and in her self-marketing. Five years younger than Beyoncé and usually considered second place in the beauty department, Solange upstaged Beyoncé in only two respects. She married and divorced first, her ex being football player Daniel Smith, and she gave birth to the first Knowles grandchild, Daniel. Unlike Beyoncé, Solange often disagrees with her father about the meaning of success, her dad's criteria being a large house and family as compared to Solange's need for contentment about her work and the fulfillment of certain goals. Solange and her sister also differ on the need for stardom. Solange cultivates privacy more than her sister does, so she realizes achieving star status may not be a reality for her. Although for many years Beyoncé let newspaper articles and people's opinions bother her, she never said anything that might alienate the public. Solange, on the other hand, is outspoken, will not tolerate gossip, and simply tells people how she feels, even if it is not diplomatic. "If someone tells me to go right, I usually go left," she said.[15] Yet Solange admires her sister and considers her a role model because she exudes sophistication and charisma.

Their dual triumphs in the same field strengthened the bond between the two sisters because they can converse about music, give each other helpful tips, network, and even perform together. During Beyoncé's acceptance speech after winning four *Billboard* awards in 2003, she thanked her sister (at that time, one of her backup singers) and told her she loved her. And when Beyoncé was on the set of *Carmen* in 2001, she expressed regret for her sister's absence. She missed Solange's nearness and habit of blasting rock music in her room. Moreover, Beyoncé paid a tribute to her sister in her autobiography: "It amazes me how you've grown into a beautiful, talented singer, songwriter, and producer at such an early age. Words can't express how proud I am of you."[16] Beyoncé believes her sister is smart and secure and able to demonstrate a sensitivity to other people's feelings while also ignoring their negative opinions. And mean-spirited gossip is something Beyoncé struggles with more than her sister, feeling especially vindictive and vengeful when people gossip about her sister or her nephew. Like a mother bird defending her babies, Beyoncé silently screeches when predators encroach on her territory and threaten those she cherishes.

FRIENDS TO THE END

Not surprisingly, Beyoncé's innate shyness precluded her from making tons of friends as a child, but once she allows someone into her inner circle, she is loyal to a fault. In elementary school her love of music and her eagerness to perform connected her to other children who felt the same, specifically Kelly Rowland, LeToya Luckett, and LaTavia Roberson. Thanks to their close working relationships, Beyoncé learned the value of women friends. Kelly and Beyoncé became inseparable while auditioning for Girl's Tyme (later called Destiny's Child) and even more so, if possible, when Tina and Mathew welcomed Kelly into their family in 1991 as a permanent guest. Kelly shared a room with Beyoncé, and many nights the two girls stayed up late giggling and swapping stories. "Our relationship got so tight after I moved in," Kelly said. "And that was the biggest blessing I could ask for."[17] Their relationship transcended their business partnership. "We have each other's back, no matter what," Beyoncé said.[18] Kelly regards Beyoncé as the same protective, nurturing nine-year-old she originally met when they both were shy and molded each other's personality for the better: Beyoncé excelled at drawing out a person's positive qualities and focusing on them; in Kelly's case, Beyoncé focused on her sense of humor and sought to improve Kelly's dancing.

In 2000, when Destiny's Child was the opening act on the Christina Aguilera Tour, Kelly struck her foot painfully against an iron ramp backstage, and Beyoncé stayed by her side to comfort her and make sure Kelly got to the emergency room for treatment. "She held my hand tight (and said), 'Don't worry, Kelly. I'm here. It's going to be okay.'"[19] To their credit, both women cultivated their friendship under often stressful circumstances, such as during Destiny's Child's breakup and the emergence of Beyoncé as a solo superstar, and as a result, they are still close allies. Kelly attended Beyoncé's wedding as did Michelle Williams and Gwyneth Paltrow.

One indicator of Beyoncé's high regard for friendship was her emotional collapse after the Destiny's Child exodus in 2000. Beyoncé had always thought of herself as a "peacemaker," but despite sincere efforts and determination, she could not resolve their conflicts and this left Beyoncé feeling frustrated and unhappy. To make matters worse, she also empathized with LaTavia and LeToya and this led to extreme stress and depression. The media fanned Beyoncé's self-flagellation by casting aspersions on Beyoncé, turning some fans against her. "A lot of people dumped everything on Beyoncé," Tina said. "They would say things to her in airports—rude evil things."[20]

Although the third member of Destiny's Child, Michelle Williams, came on the scene relatively late in the group's history, Beyoncé and she became friends quickly. Similar backgrounds—a two-parent home in a middle-class suburb, an emphasis on education, and a love of music and church—drew them together, but they did not bond overnight. It took time for the positive vibes to gel into a firm friendship, then a sisterly devotion. Beyoncé cherished these female relationships so much that she remained absolute in her rejection of any guy who made disparaging remarks about her two longtime friends. These relationships were inviolable to her and had to be respected as such, and any male needed to understand those boundaries. "Anyone who has two true friends in this life is very lucky," Beyoncé wrote. "And if you have more than that, you are truly blessed." [21] Beyoncé values friendship, but caution tells her that friendships and the world of entertainment do not necessarily mix. Her insight and maturity have proved to her that many so-called friends cannot handle another person's success and their negative attitude reflects low self-esteem and not an indictment of Beyoncé.

Fortunately, Beyoncé has a few similar-age relatives such as her second cousin, Kenric, who worked for Tina's salon, Headliners, and Beyoncé's first cousin, Angela Beyince, who has been Beyoncé's personal assistant for a number of years. Angela co-authored many songs with Beyoncé and Destiny's Child. "You are not only one of my best friends, you are like the big sister I never had," Beyoncé said to her in 2002.[22]

WORSHIP FROM AFAR

Growing up, Beyoncé looked to celebrity role models, among them Diana Ross, Whitney Houston, Janet Jackson, Tina Turner, Madonna, Barbra Streisand, Aaliyah, Anita Baker, Aretha Franklin, Mariah Carey, and Michael Jackson. Beyoncé admired Madonna not only for her musical style, but also for her business sense—the way she turned negatives into positives. In 2000, when an overwhelmed and nervous Destiny's Child sang at the Grammys, Beyoncé walked down the steps onto the stage and saw Madonna staring back in the audience. Beyoncé clutched the railing for dear life and wondered what she was doing there. Although Madonna's presence intimidated Beyoncé, it maximized Destiny's Child's performance.

Beyoncé has gotten to know many of her role models. She met Diana Ross at *VH1's Divas 2000: A Tribute to Diana Ross* and was overcome with emotion. Another heroine, Stevie Nicks, appeared in Destiny's Child's 2004 "Bootylicious" video, when Nicks advised the group to avoid the burnout common in the entertainment industry. Another "hero from afar" meeting took place at Whitney Houston's birthday party in New York City in 1998, at which time the girls discovered that Houston was a big fan. She wanted to hug them, but all the girls could manage was to stare back in awe. At the BET Awards in 2001, when Houston sang "I Will Always Love You," she pointed at Destiny's Child while vocalizing the line, "I hope life treats you kind." Beyoncé met every singer she ever loved and got to perform onstage with Michael Jackson. It did not get any better than that.

Beyoncé also made a connection with the singer Aaliyah, whom she met at an awards show, then later saw at a Destiny's Child rehearsal for a 1998 video shoot of "Get on the Bus." Although Destiny's Child was relatively new on the scene and Aaliyah had big-time hits, she took the time to visit with the group and help them rewind their tape. Beyoncé and she became friends for a short while and went sightseeing and shopping around Los Angeles. "She was definitely an angel," Beyoncé said.[23] In 2001, Aaliyah died in an airplane accident.

Beyoncé always took away something from her relationships, even when they were short-lived like her acquaintance with Aaliyah. She could not help but notice that both Mariah Carey and Diana Ross progressed in the entertainment field after appearances in the films *Glitter* and *Mahogany*, respectively. These observations helped her later on when she had to decide on the career merits of Hollywood.

ROMANTIC RELATIONSHIPS

While growing up, Beyoncé spent much more time watching music videos of groups like En Vogue than chasing boys, and since her mother prohibited dating until she was 16, romance proved elusive for a while. But around age 12, Beyoncé became interested in a boy a few years older than she. "I thought I was in love," she wrote.[24] Beyoncé and Kelly went to a party at his house, where Beyoncé found out he was dating someone else and that he thought Beyoncé was too young and naïve.

HIGH-SCHOOL ROMANCE

At age 14, Beyoncé met Lindell, two years her senior and someone she dated for six years. The two talked regularly on the phone, and Lindell visited at Beyoncé's house once a week. One of their first dates was at the Water Wall near the Galleria Mall in Houston, but Beyoncé took things slowly (although Kelly encouraged her to be more demonstrative) and did not kiss Lindell until she was in eighth grade. Because Beyoncé was scared and shy about romance, she and Lindell were hanging around a Jack in the Box on the day Beyoncé finally got up the courage to kiss him. Afterwards she felt extremely embarrassed. "I told Kelly, 'Oh, man, that sucked,'"

Beyoncé wrote.[25] Then Beyoncé's cousin found out what Beyoncé had done, and Beyoncé worried that her cousin would tell her parents.

Beyoncé went to Lindell's prom, but being only 16, she had an early curfew. The relationship continued even after Beyoncé left high school to begin her recording career, but it suffered because of the long separations. Another problem was that Beyoncé hid her recording career from Lindell for a long time, and he believed she played the piano for a music group. Once Lindell learned about Beyoncé and Destiny's Child, the relationship cooled because, for Beyoncé, career was a priority. "I'm lucky we are still friends," Beyoncé said in 2001. "His friendship is very special and important to me."[26]

After Lindell, Beyoncé found it difficult to meet someone new since she was either on the road or in the studio. She also began to distrust guys' intentions and wondered if they were attracted to her fame or her personality. It was hard for her to open up to guys when in the back of her mind, she questioned if they really liked her or her celebrity status. "I'd love to have a boyfriend," Beyoncé said in 2001. "If I could find a boyfriend that could put up with this life, that would be great."[27] By the time she was 22, Beyoncé's views on dating had solidified: "When women are in a relationship," she said, "even if the man is trifling or cheating and he's wrong and ignores you and you end up not wanting him, the thought of another woman benefiting from what you taught him kills you."[28]

DANGEROUSLY IN LOVE

The next time Beyoncé began a serious relationship with a guy she chose someone from the entertainment world—someone even more famous than she: rapper Shawn Corey Carter, better known as Jay-Z. Beyoncé first got to know the founder of Def Jam Recordings, Roc-A-Fella, and RocaWear in 2003, when the two recorded the duet "Bonnie and Clyde" for Jay-Z's *The Blueprint: the Gift and the Curse* album. Released as a single, the song took off, and so did the relationship, even though Jay-Z, who is rumored to be worth between approximately $300 million and $500 million,[29] was 11 years older than Beyoncé. Soon the twosome started showing up and being photographed at fashion shows, the Z-100 Jingle Ball, basketball games and parties, consistently demanding privacy on the subjects of romance and marriage. "We don't play with our relationship," Jay-Z said.[30]

Gradually Beyoncé got to know the good, the bad, and the ugly of this high priest of hip-hop. Jay-Z, the youngest of five children, was born on December 4, 1969, and grew up in the Bedford-Stuyvesant area of Brooklyn—the low-income, high-crime "Marcy" apartment projects that reeked of drugs, guns, and welfare lists. His parents (Gloria Carter, an investment company clerk, and Adnes Reeves) were both obsessed with music, but although crates of records were stacked up around the apartment, his parents' musical tastes differed so widely that they never shared their passion. At age nine, Jay-Z witnessed the murder of a neighbor and realized he could be next if he stayed long in the 'hood. Three years later, his father left home and distanced himself from the family. "The person I looked up to most was my father," Jay-Z said, "and once I experienced that hurt from the guy you thought was superman, you never want to feel that hurt again."[31] The result: From then on, Jay-Z avoided close relationships and emotional communication until the death of his father in 2003 inspired him to open up more to people, especially Beyoncé.

By his late teens, Jay-Z lived and breathed music, had dropped out of high school, and was dealing drugs, specifically crack cocaine. Already an entrepreneur of sorts, he juggled numbers and memorized accounts for his clients; at the same time, he exercised his talents, generating musical rhymes and rappings, carrying around a green notebook in which he constantly jotted down rhymes and verses. His musical strengths gravitated toward catchy beats, sing-song hooks and rhymes, but try as he might, Shawn Corey the rapper could not transform himself into Jay-Z the recording star, at least not yet. Because no one knew the ambitious 25-year-old well enough to record him, in 1995 Jay-Z started Roc-A-Fella Records with his two friends, Damon Dash and Kareem Burke. Jay-Z's first marketing strategy was selling albums out of a car trunk, and with a label and innate talent, it did not take the Brooklyn native long to record seven multiplatinum albums in a row. "The funny thing is," Jay-Z said, "I never wanted to be famous. I had the sense of being famous before I was famous."[32]

In December 1999, Jay-Z, at age 30, became famous again—notorious, really—after assaulting two people at a local nightclub. He allegedly stabbed fellow rap mogul Lance Rivera and crashed a bottle over another patron's head. Rivera may have bootlegged some of the rapper's music, as alleged, but whatever perpetrated the argument, Jay-Z was arrested and in the criminal justice system. "It was the dumbest thing I ever did," Jay-Z said about the attacks[33] to which he pleaded guilty to third-degree misdemeanor assault and was sentenced to three years probation. Jay-Z also settled a civil law suit (stemming from the altercation) out of court for between $500,000 and $1 million.[34] "You work hard for years, and it can all go away in a night," Jay-Z said.[35]

Nowadays Jay-Z fraternizes with many of the most well-educated, financially flush power brokers in New York. A dapper dresser with a smooth, self-confident air, he learned all he needed in the bloody battlegrounds of the city's projects: "I learnt about integrity, sticking by your word and taking chances," he said.[36] Jay-Z's politics influence millions of his younger fans, so his meeting and chat with 2008 Democratic presidential candidate Barack Obama, who remarked how much he liked the rapper's *American Gangster* album and Beyoncé's show, was premeditated, publicized by the media, and aimed at getting the attention of younger voters.

THE MARRYING KIND

Love for Beyoncé demands privacy as well as surrender—even in high school she remained tight-lipped about relationships. "I only talk about them in songwriting; otherwise things get too messy," she said.[37] Through her music she expressed the sentiments that love made people vulnerable to pain, which is why it was dangerous. People yielded everything over to another person, knowing that person might manipulate the other's feelings through word and deed.

In 1999, before meeting Jay-Z, Beyoncé said she wanted a man who accepted her and was not egotistical or obsessed with money—a man who respected God, women in general, and her in particular. She knew a confident family-minded man would help her grow. "I don't like guys who walk in a room and want a lot of attention," she said.[38] Instead, men should impress a woman with their personality—their intelligence, for instance, elegance and laid-back attitude. Beyoncé expected a man to treat problems pragmatically and dispassionately and find a way to resolve them, to use conflict management and to aim for good communication, true friendship, and laughter. Because she tours a great deal, she needed someone who could share intimacies and daily activities over the telephone.

RUMOR MILL

Because of the couple's extroverted, high-profile lifestyle, Beyoncé and Jay-Z have been magnets for the press. Gossip surrounded the couple since they began dating, with rumors circulated about engagements, pregnancies, or secret marriages pouring out of the pages of tabloids and Internet sites alike. Tina tried to kill several of the more inflammatory rumors, such as that Jay-Z planned to become Beyoncé's new manager or that Tina intended to divorce Mathew and take over as manager, but to no avail. Generally, Beyoncé and Jay-Z, who got matching tattoos of the number four on their ring fingers[39] (their birthdays and wedding anniversary are on the fourth days of various months), do not comment on rumors (except to express their distaste for the lies and pain caused to others), and this has evolved to the point that they delayed months in confirming their marriage, although reporters searched the public records and found that in April 2008, the couple filed for a marriage license in Scarsdale, New York.

But even before her relationship with Jay-Z, Beyoncé clashed with the tabloid press, which at various times called her a bitch, a diva, a fatty, and, conversely, an anorexic, and reported that her father had numerous affairs and a serious drug problem. Rumors bother Beyoncé more than anything else because "You're only one person, you can't even defend yourself," she said.[40] Now that Beyoncé is married, the rumors can only multiply, with the gossip mill churning out regular announcements of pregnancies, miscarriages, abortions, separations, divorces, adoptions, quarrels, domestic abuse, and, yes, extraterrestrial visitations.

NOTES

1. Quoted in "Gayle King Interviews . . . On the Road with Destiny's Child," *Business Wire*, November 27, 2001, www.thefreelibrary.com (accessed July 7, 2008).

2. Quoted in "The Music Issue: Beyoncé Knowles," *Texas Monthly*, April 2004, www.texasmonthly.com (accessed May 8, 2008).

3. Quoted by Terri Dougherty, *Beyoncé* (New York: Lucent Books/Thomson Gale, 2007), 66.

4. Quoted by Lynn Norment, "Tina & Mathew Knowles Created the Destiny's Child Gold Mine," *Ebony*, September 2001, www.findarticles.com (accessed June 6, 2008).

5. Quoted in Jenny Eliscu, "Beyoncé Knowles of Destiny's Child," *Rolling Stone*, July 6, 2000, www.ebscohost.com (accessed July 1, 2008).

6. Quoted by Lisa Robinson, "Above and Beyoncé," *Vanity Fair*, November 2005, www.accessmylibrary.com (accessed June 6, 2008).

7. Quoted by Amy Longsdorf, "Beyoncé's Dream Role," *Herald Sun*, January 13, 2007, www.news.com.au (accessed June 12, 2008).

8. Quoted by Norment.

9. Quoted by Toure, "Beyoncé," *Rolling Stone*, March 4, 2004, www.ebscohost.com (accessed June 6, 2008).

10. Quoted by Mark Anthony Neal, "Beyoncé: Dangerously in Love," www.popmatters.com (accessed June 6, 2008).

11. "Author: Strong Fathers Make 'Fearless' Daughters," November 7, 2007, www.npr.org (accessed September 7, 2008).

12. Quoted by VH1 web site on Beyoncé, www.vh1.com (accessed June 6, 2006).

13. Quoted by Dougherty, 48.

14. Quoted in "The Music Issue."

15. Quoted by Jeanine Edwards, "Solange Knowles: Flying Solo," *Essence*, October 2007, www.essence.com (accessed June 6, 2008).

16. Quoted in Beyoncé Knowles, Kelly Rowland, and Michelle Williams, *Soul Survivors: The Official Autobiography of Destiny's Child* (New York: Regan Books, 2002), 279.

17. Quoted in Knowles et al., 51.

18. Quoted by Rosa Waters, *Beyoncé* (Broomall, PA: Mason Crest, 2007), 27.

19. Quoted in Knowles et al., 184.

20. Quoted in "The Music Issue."

21. Quoted in Knowles et al., 229.

22. Quoted in Knowles et al., 279.

23. Quoted in Knowles et al., 221.

24. Knowles et al., 61.

25. Knowles et al., 62.

26. Quoted in Knowles et al., 73.

27. Quoted in Paul Goldsmith, "Destiny's Child," *TexasMusic*, Winter 2001, 45.

28. Quoted in Scott Paulson Bryant, "Beyoncé: If I Was Your Girlfriend," *Giant Magazine*, December 6, 2007, www.giantmag.com (accessed June 28, 2008).

29. "Rapper Jay-Z Decides to boycott Cristal . . ." June 15, 2006, www.newsvine.com (accessed September 7, 2008).

30. Quoted in Michelle Tauber and Lauren Comander, "The Good Life," *People*, October 25, 2004, www. Ebscohost.com (accessed June 12, 2008).

31. Quoted in "Father's Death Makes Jay-Z a Better Boyfriend," *Wenn*, November 30, 2007, www.thefreelibrary.com (accessed June 19, 2008).

32. Ibid.

33. Ibid.

34. Ibid.

35. Quoted by Josh Tyrangiel, "In His Next Lifetime," *Time*, November 24, 2003, www.time.com (accessed June 6, 2008).

36. Quoted by Carl Wilkinson, "Exclusive Jay-Z Interview: I'm with the Brand," *Financial Times*, November 4, 2006, www.carlwilkinson.co.uk (accessed May 22, 2008).

37. Quoted by Dougherty 86.

38. Quoted by Jeannine Amber, "A Fashionable Life," *Essence*, September 2006, www.highbeam.com (accessed June 19, 2008).

39. Jeannine Amber, "I Am Legend," *Essence*, November 2008, www.web. ebscohost.com. (accessed November 24, 2008).

40. Quoted by MSN/BET Chat, www.msn.com (accessed June 6, 2008).

Chapter 9

ME-DIA, MYSELF, AND I

Celebrities work hard at creating public images because they want to give their fans and the media a carefully orchestrated view of their personality and positive character traits. That often means hiring publicists and public relations agencies to circulate press releases that portray celebrities in specific, easily packaged ways, for example, the celebrity as environmentalist, the celebrity as genius (Mensa member), and the celebrity as recovered substance abuser and adoring father.

Public image normally differs to some degree from the person's real self (how a person perceives himself/herself) and the ideal self (what he or she would like to be), but these psychodynamic concepts have one thing in common: they are in flux, volatile, and reactive to the outer and inner environments. Personal observations and media feedback can give the average person insight into a celebrity's public image; for instance, Beyoncé's image can be discerned from an examination of her actions and interactions with numerous reporters, photographers, employees, colleagues, and fans, but her admissions to journalists and her demeanor and body language account for only a partial picture of the superstar. That perception is precisely what the famous singer and her publicists want fans and others to accept as fact. For instance, when a photographer at a 2004 photo shoot asked Beyoncé to remove her hand from her hips, the reporter noted she shook her head no and said, "My hips are too big," then giggled and asked, "Can't I just smile?"[1] In this example, Beyoncé portrayed herself as shy and self-critical—a woman not particularly glib and extremely self-conscious of her shape and the public's judgment of that fact.

PUBLIC FACE

Beyoncé has carefully crafted the public image that she wishes to telegraph to her audience. She has a track record of grumbling to the press about her weight and eating habits in a convincing I-am-an-average-woman manner that makes her sound 20 pounds overweight and totally fixated on pizza and ice cream. Another time, before a photo shoot for the October 2005 cover of *Vanity Fair,* Beyoncé put herself on a low-carb weight-loss diet, and the public read how Kelly and Michelle cooperated by not eating pizza in front of her. Although Beyoncé says she struggles with the weight issue, at other times she demonstrates the practiced discipline of the professional calorie counter. *Vanity Fair* reporter Lisa Robinson watched Beyoncé exhibit admirable will power at a dessert-laden Grammy party in February 2005. "If you cut little slices it's not so bad," Beyoncé said, motioning toward a tray of rich treats.[2] Another interviewer bluntly asked the singer if she tired of "putting on" the Beyoncé "character" in public.[3] He then learned that Beyoncé adorned herself in wild clothes and eye-catching bling for photo shoots and videos only, but at home she skipped the jewels, the stiletto heels, and makeup. That may actually be the *real* Beyoncé *or* it may be only her public image—what she wants us to believe—but one way to probe this is to look for moments when she drops her guard. In a 2003 interview, for example, Beyoncé momentarily forgot herself and began cracking her knuckles until she noticed this habit was not part of her acceptable code of behavior for her public image. That same year Beyoncé agreed to an interview and dinner at a reporter's Brooklyn house, where the writer heard her exchange intimacies with her mother, father, and sister while Beyoncé relaxed on a pillow on the living room floor. For this brief interlude, her worries about family members appeared genuine and her sensitivity real and unforced.

Another way to determine a person's credibility is to ask someone knowledgeable about Beyoncé and her behind-the-scenes behavior—someone like choreographer Frank Gatson, who has seen the many emotional faces of Beyoncé.

"You wanna think she's a b—— because she's so fine," Gatson said in 2004.[4] Beyoncé gets angry when it's appropriate, but she holds back her temper because she knows self-control gives her an advantage. So she smiles politely and rolls her eyes instead of unleashing her emotions. Although she lives like a queen, she does not act in an affected way. Beyoncé also ignores negative feedback from the audience when she is onstage and appears fearless because she does not react to booing or other obvious criticisms. Instead, Beyoncé dismisses her nervousness and anger and opts for a constructive path to release pent-up feelings. A practical young woman, she makes an effort to reframe problems so the solutions work to her benefit.

THE 'ISMS

Beyoncé takes advantage of her high-profile status for humanitarian causes she supports, as in 2005, when along with other rich and famous entertainment personalities, Beyoncé appeared on TV to do an "I am a Jew" public service announcement for the New York-based Foundation for Ethnic Understanding. With the encouragement of friend Russell Simmons of record label Def Jam and her then-boyfriend Jay-Z, Beyoncé told people to reject anti-Semitism, alerting the public to instances of prejudice against Jews.

Surprisingly, she does not use the media as a platform to preach against racism. But there's a good explanation for that, according to Ellis Cashmore, professor at Staffordshire University in the United Kingdom. Cashmore argues that Beyoncé and other black celebrities such as Bill Cosby, Oprah Winfrey, Michael Jordan, Will Smith, Sean Combs, Snoop Dogg, and Whoopi Goldberg embrace the great god money while they deny racism's influence on modern society.[5] Cashmore presented this theory in an academic paper, *Buying Beyoncé: the Deal that Ended Racism*, at a 2005 conference in the United Kingdom. Cashmore said Beyoncé represents the new twenty-first century celebrity who, by virtue of her accomplishments, demonstrates that prejudice no longer presents a barrier to success.[6] Beyoncé reiterated this on September 7, 2006, when journalist Diane Sawyer, of ABC News, questioned Beyoncé about racism's role in her career. The star acknowledged the legacies of black pioneers, but summed up by saying, "Now no one's paying attention to what race I am, I'm past that."[7]

Colorblindness may be the prevailing attitude of the music industry and the media, but not everyone approves of multiracialism. Columbia University history professor Barbara Fields said, "Such a view, for the aura of progressivism and righteousness that currently surround multiracialism, is not a cure for racism but a particularly ugly manifestation of it."[8] In short, Fields meant that when Beyoncé disputed the use of a colored lens through which people view others, she drew attention to that "racial filter" and its correlation with inferiority.

POLITICALLY CORRECT

In an effort to become politically correct and prevent serious injury to her public image, Beyoncé changed her position on fur. At least as far back as 2002, PETA (People for the Ethical Treatment of Animals) has been chastising Beyoncé about her decision to wear fur garments. Then, when her fashion company, House of Dereon, started adding fur to its fashions in 2004, Beyoncé found herself in the center of an animal-rights controversy. It was not until DNA tests proved that much of the China-imported fur came from domestic dogs that Beyoncé stopped the use of fur in her apparel.

FEAR OF FAILURE

The PETA debacle gave fans a peek into how Beyoncé's public and real images often clash. Although public reaction disrupted Beyoncé's equilibrium, she also reaped something positive from the brouhaha. Beyoncé ultimately changed her position, not because the demands of political correctness forced her, but because her business was possibly an unknowing accomplice to a morally indefensible action. This is the unaffected behavior of a basically honest person who at various times candidly admitted to pain in her wisdom teeth and lower back and also complained of a stuffy nose. But Beyoncé carefully controls the extent of her natural emotional reactions to discomfort, refraining from being sulky, irritable, or stubborn lest these displays tarnish her public image.

Sincerity marks a person as authentic, and it can go a long way toward preserving a public image. When Beyoncé was with Destiny's Child, she openly acknowledged her fear of solo performances. "It takes courage to step out on your own," Beyoncé said.[9] She described the comfort of remaining in a group, knowing that her colleagues faced the same nervousness, pressures, and gossip as she did. The security of joint decision making and the specter of failure in the film industry also scared her because it was a new medium. "You just always have to take risks," she said, challenging her fears.[10]

At age 27, Beyoncé continues to test her limits, assess her capabilities, and craft her public image; one moment she appears terrified of overreaching her talents, the next moment supremely confident of them. Movie producer John Lyons, who hired Beyoncé for the *Austin Powers* film, compared her to Barbra Streisand, who by virtue of her artistic accomplishments in music, movie direction, and acting, is often considered a "Renaissance woman." "You just know she (Beyoncé) can do anything and have this amazing career," Lyons said.[11] Husband Jay-Z agrees and recognizes his wife as one of the best singers today; *Cosmopolitan* praised Beyoncé for her risk taking, boldness, and independence in reaching her goals, naming her 2006 Fun Fearless Female of the Year. *Cosmopolitan* also recognized her healthy ego. ("I think that I'm a natural-born leader," Beyoncé said, also acknowledging her physical attractiveness.[12]) At the same time, she projected a gee-golly-whiz air of humility in front of an audience of adolescent girls in Washington, D.C. at a 2007 conference. "I have insecurities, things I don't like about myself," she said.[13] Despite her frailties, however, Beyoncé admits she needs to keep testing herself. "If something's easy, the excitement is gone," she said. "I don't like to be bored, and I don't like to be comfortable."[14]

WHO IS THE REAL BEYONCÉ?

Some fans doubt Beyoncé's authenticity because she appears to take the so-called comfortable path in her performances, for example, relying on sexual innuendo instead of her vocal abilities. Many of Beyoncé's fans and critics decry that need because she relates to fans appropriately when offstage. If fans approach her for autographs or other favors, she does not ooze sex goddess or Amazon-princess; she presents herself as more the artist than the promiscuous female or Madonna-whore archetype. As the nursery rhyme goes, "When she was good, she was very, very good, and when she was bad, she was awful." Onstage, Beyoncé might be that sinful lady, but around 1999, when a fan requested an autograph immediately after Beyoncé learned a close relative had died, she wrote, "I had to pretend everything was ok and wipe the tears from my eyes, get on my feet, sign the autograph, and smile."[15]

BECOMING BEYONCÉ

No one can predict the trajectory a person's life can take, even the individual herself. Although a mature personality remains relatively stable, events can and do impact a person and cause ripples extending outward. A traumatic divorce, a deceitful spouse, or an unexpected epiphany can set a person on a new course, as it did with secretary-turned-zoologist Jane Goodall (who studied chimpanzees) and physician-turned-writer Michael Crichton (who authored medical thrillers and created TV's *ER*). Each abandoned his or her first profession and followed another dream— Beyoncé surely has had moments of doubt since as far back as 2001, when she recognized the stress of the music industry and her fear of overdoing it and harming her health. She sustained vocal injuries from frequently singing lead parts and hardly had time to "enjoy the blessings" (such as an award) because of her busy schedule.[16]

And there is also something called ambition, which Beyoncé wants to pursue, as she aspires to be on the entertainment scene for the next 20 years. In 2004, she earned a place in the London branch of Madame Tussaud's Wax Museum, so there's no stopping Beyoncé. Longevity translates to pressure in the entertainment world—an industry notorious for insecurity—where a film star can take a two-week vacation and return to find her dressing room and wardrobe cleared out. Beyoncé knows other young women are already lining up to replace her, so staying on top is crucial. "You have to know that yeah, you might be talented, you might work hard, but it can all be taken away," she said.[17]

Beyoncé's maturity and self-discipline, however, may give her the staying power she craves, but she also knows luck and shifting priorities can work the other way, as happened to Jen Trynin, a singer-songwriter of the 1990s. Trynin's self-produced CD became a local hit and the singer went on tour and made it into the pages of Rolling Stone. But when her second CD failed to score big, her agent lost interest in her. Trynin reassessed her life and decided to end her music career. Although Beyoncé says she wants to remain an entertainer for a while, she often refers or alludes to a quieter, more conventional life to which she would retire to paint or teach an art class or "maybe one day sell paintings for charity—if they are good enough!"[18]

ACTIONS SPEAK LOUDER THAN WORDS

Like most people, however, Beyoncé's actions say more about her than her rhetoric. In February 2008, Beyoncé honored 1960s legend Tina Turner, and the two performed the classic "Proud Mary" at the 2007 Grammy Awards. The audience thrilled to the raucous duet, but praise from critics was later spoiled by Aretha Franklin's anger over Beyoncé's introduction of Tina Turner as the "Queen of Soul."

Beyoncé's words were not intended to be controversial, but the minute they tumbled out of her mouth they became as provocative as are her recent forays into bluegrass and Latin music and her continued exploration of dramatic movie roles. Beyoncé sang the bluegrass and Hispanic versions of "Irreplaceable" with the country band Sugarland and plays blues singer Etta James in the 2008 movie Cadillac Records. The film, which co-stars Adrien Brody, tells the story of Chicago's Chess Records (the label's artists included Chuck Berry and Muddy Waters) and its founder, Leonard Chess, who started selling albums out of his Cadillac. James, who recorded the standard "At Last" consulted with Beyoncé during the filming to add greater authenticity and insight to the material because James claimed she smoked in the bathroom in school and was arrogant. "I kinda have a man's voice. It's a contralto, more bluesy, religious," she said.[19] Later in 2008, Beyoncé took another step, starring in the thriller, *Obsessed,* in which she plays a beautiful wife married to an asset manager who is stalked by a temporary office worker. She also recorded a new album.

Judging by her busy schedule, Beyoncé intends to continue challenging herself, and even if she "retires," it may only be temporary or a prelude to another ambitious project because although she has won many Grammys, she still hopes to win an Oscar and Tony, too. "As soon as you accomplish one thing, it's not enough," she said, echoing Hollywood's mantra that you are as good as your last job.[20] By the looks of it, Beyoncé is not slowing down, even in her personal life, since she married longtime beau Jay-Z on April 4, 2008 in his Tribeca penthouse in Manhattan. The couple celebrated that evening with 50 or so close friends and family, but separated the next day to return to work—the groom to continue touring with singer Mary Blige and the bride to finish filming *Cadillac Records*. Despite the power of the press and pressure from fans, Beyoncé appears to be becoming herself more and more with each passing day.

NOTES

1. Quoted in "The Music Issue: Beyoncé Knowles," *Texas Monthly,* April 2004, www.texasmonthly.com (accessed May 11, 2008).

2. Quoted by Terri Dougherty, *Beyoncé* (New York: Lucent/Thomson Gale, 2007), 74.

3. Quoted in "Beyoncé Knowles' Different Destiny," ivillage.co.uk (accessed April 18, 2008).

4. Quoted by Toure, "Cover Story: A Woman Possessed," *Rolling Stone,* March 4, 2004, www.rollingstone.com (accessed April 18, 2008).

5. Shirley English, "End of Racism Is Corporate Mirage," *The Times,* September 14, 2005, www.timesonline.co.uk (accessed April 18, 2008).

6. Ibid.

7. Quoted by Justina Sade Williams, "Beyoncé in Limbo: The Contortions and Back Bending of Black Femininity," University of California at Irvine, Undergraduate Research Paper, 2006, www.web.due.uci.edu (accessed June 6, 2008).

8. Quoted by Barbara J. Fields, "Of Rogues and Geldings," *The American Historical Review*, 2003, 1402.

9. Quoted in "Beyoncé: Fun, Fearless Woman of the Year 2006," www.cosmopolitan.com/celebrities/exclusive/beyoncé-interview-2 (accessed June 12, 2008).

10. "Beyoncé and Patrick Dempsey Named Cosmopolitan's 2006 Fun Fearless Female and Male of the Year," *Business Wire*, January 13, 2006, www.thefreelibrary.com (accessed June 17, 2008).

11. Quoted by Allison Samuels, "What Beyoncé Wants," *Newsweek*, July 29, 2002, www.newsweek.com (accessed June 8, 2008).

12. Billy Johnson, Jr., "Destiny Awaits," May 27, 2004, www.music.yahoo.com (accessed June 8, 2008).

13. Quoted by Jodi Lynn Bryson, "Ooh, Child: Destiny Talks," *Teen Magazine*, August 2001, www.ebscohost.com (accessed April 16, 2008).

14. Quoted in Scott Paulson Bryant, "Beyoncé: If I Was Your Girlfriend," *Giant Magazine*, December 6, 2007, www.giantmag.com (accessed July 2, 2008).

15. Quoted in Beyoncé Knowles, Kelly Rowland, and Michelle Williams, *Soul Survivors: The Official Autobiography of Destiny's Child* (New York: Regan/HarperCollins, 2002), 230.

16. Quoted by Geoff Boucher, "Destiny, Manifest," *Los Angeles Times*, July 1, 2001, //web.lexis.com (accessed June 12, 2008).

17. Quoted by Dougherty, 62.

18. Quoted in "All I Want for Christmas . . .," *Sunday life (Belfast, Northern Ireland)*, December 24, 2006, www.belfasttelegraph.co.uk (accessed April 18, 2008).

19. Quoted by Janee Bolden, "Beyoncé Too 'Bougie' for Etta James Role?" *The Wire/Daily Hip-Hop News*, February 25, 2008, www.sohh.com (accessed April 18, 2008).

20. Quoted by Simon Garfield, "Uh-Oh, Uh-Oh, Uh-Oh," *The Guardian*, December 14, 2003, www.arts.guardian.co.uk (accessed June 8, 2008).

Destiny's Child arrives at the event "VH1 Divas 2000: A Tribute to Diana Ross" in 2000 in New York. AP Photo/Tina Fineberg.

Beyoncé and then-boyfriend Jay-Z perform together during the Sixth Annual BET Awards in 2006 in Los Angeles. AP Images.

As part of the Beyoncé Experience 2007 World Tour, Beyoncé performs in concert in Shanghai in 2007. AP Images.

Beyoncé is interviewed on the Tonight Show with Jay Leno in 2007. AP Images.

Beyoncé and Tina Turner perform at the 50th Annual Grammy Awards in 2008 in Los Angeles. AP Photo/Kevork Djansezian.

Chapter 10

BACKING UP BEYONCÉ

Star performers in touring shows seldom appear onstage by themselves; their acts usually include instrumentalists, dancers, and vocal backup. But backup never means second-rate because it refers to musical and choreographic virtuosos who have trained and practiced for years for the opportunity to appear with headliners such as Beyoncé. They are the "cream of the crop" and know how to make great performers look spectacular.

Beyoncé knows the importance of backup performers and how vital it is to maintain good relationships with them so that support staff feel positive about their contributions. On tour, these musicians and dancers sometimes spend more time with Beyoncé than close friends and family members. Besides meeting for practice sessions and performances, recreational activities sometimes bring the entire company together; for example, during *The 2007 Beyoncé Experience Tour*, Beyoncé rented out a roller rink for her staff's enjoyment and relaxation. But because Beyoncé socializes with her employees does not mean permission is thereby granted to upstage her during performances. In fact, if there is any one golden rule among backup artists, it is that no one out-sings or out-dances the star.

DANCIN', DANCIN'

Beyoncé gets high marks for her dancing, so her backups need to be every bit as good, if not more accomplished, than she. Watch any Las Vegas or Broadway performance and you will observe that the choreography sometimes is so complex and fast-paced that you wonder how any dancer can execute all the moves so quickly. The Frank Gatsons—both father and junior—have choreographed much of the dance sequences for Destiny's Child and Beyoncé. They also help conduct auditions and weed out the less agile dancers, for only the best performers can do justice to the choreography.

Every choreographer seeks certain qualities in dancers while conducting auditions. For Destiny's Child's backup dancers, the criteria included height, an athletic body, and the ability to internalize the correct vibes and project them outward. Gatson also looked for dancers with backgrounds in ballet, jazz, and hip-hop. Cincinnati, Ohio-based dancer Byron Carter was hired in the summer of 2005 for the Destiny's Child's *Destiny Fulfilled* tour and also appeared in Beyoncé's 2007 *The Beyoncé Experience* tour. Other former backup dancers include Clyph McGhee, a choreographer and performer in Beyoncé's "Get Me Bodied" video; Tyrell Washington, a dancer proficient in hip-hop, break dancing, modern dance, and African dance; Anthony Burrell, a member of the Alvin Ailey American Dance Theater; Heather Morris, a member of Beyoncé's 2007 North American tour; and Ashley Everett, a 16-year veteran of hip-hop and ballet and one of four new dancers hired for Beyoncé's 2007 World Tour. More recently, Mathew hired Ashley Shaw of Sheffield, England, as a backup singer/dancer for a future Beyoncé tour. Formerly with the all-girl R&B act, From Above, Shaw, 18, was spotted at a London showcase and signed a contract with Beyoncé in June 2008.

CHOREOGRAPHERS

All choreographers listen to the music first before brainstorming dance moves. "You may have some type of movement in mind, but you definitely have to listen . . . to find if the dance moves fit with the music," Frank Gatson said.[1] For the *Destiny Fulfilled* album, Gatson, who with LaVelle Smith Jr. earned five MTV awards for Best Choreography for his contributions to the "Naughty Girl" video, auditioned many male dancers throughout the United States. Beyoncé has worked with several choreographers besides Gatson; among them are Junella Segura, Lavelle Smith Jr., and Fatima Robinson. Robinson, who choreographs for other artists besides Beyoncé (including the Backstreet Boys and Nelly Furtado), directed the Destiny's Child "Bootylicious" video. Before working on that project, Robinson listened to the music multiple times to stimulate her creativity, then watched Beyoncé perform so that Robinson could pick up on her unique style. Smith, a graduate of the Youth Performing Arts School in Louisville, Kentucky, who performed and/or choreographed for Diana Ross, Janet Jackson, TLC, Texas, and En Vogue, as well as accompanied dancers on three Michael Jackson tours, put together Beyoncé's "Get Me Bodied" video. The world-famous choreographer has never become flustered and awed by Beyoncé and other famous performers while working, but afterwards, when he hung out with those same celebrities, "It would hit me. I can't believe that I'm sitting here with this person."[2] Junella Segura Cooper also choreographed for Beyoncé, as well as McHammer, Ciara, Mary Blige, and Destiny's Child. In 2007–2008, Cooper taught dance at the Tupac Amaru Shakur Foundation in Stone Mountain, Georgia, as well as at a summer camp in Atlanta.

Beyoncé mixes in hip-hop with her routines so she also needed the expertise of Tabitha and Napoleon D'umo, who have consulted with Destiny's Child, Monica, and Missy Elliott. The D'umos, who practice hours to perform dance tricks such as balancing, have a hip-hop style that combines jazz funk with "lock and pop and cranking to produce a raw LA commercial style."[3] Tabitha and her partner never expected to dance professionally, but the TV show "American Idol" spurred them to build up a clientele because the program galvanized the dance community. Choreographers must invent steps to convey tone as the singers vocalize.

AUDITIONS

In 2003, Beyoncé sat beside Frank Gatson and LaVelle Smith while the two choreographers and their star performer auditioned more than 800 dancers for Beyoncé's "Crazy in Love" video. "The beat is so hard it hurts your heart when you listen to it," Beyoncé said about her fast-paced hit single[4] with its extravagant use of horns. Beyoncé wanted to give as many people as possible the opportunity to audition because she felt the excitement of auditions pumped up the company and benefited the entire ensemble. Like Gatson, she looked for that indescribable magic that an enthusiastic, skilled dancer conveys, but Beyoncé also wanted to make sure no "divas" were hired. "I don't want anybody who's going to cause any drama," she said, adding that uncooperative dancers need not apply.[5]

IN STILETTO HEELS

Whatever the choreography, Beyoncé dances in extremely high heels, seemingly carrying off every sequence adeptly and joyfully. Dancers know that complicated moves in heels are possible if you hold your stomach in tightly, but in a video from Beyoncé's 2007 North American tour, dancers managed their stilettos by grabbing onto an overhead bar not seen in the video. What is more difficult for Beyoncé than dancing in heels is dancing and singing at the same time because Beyoncé and the other dancers need to be in tip-top physical shape and properly hydrated or else they tire quickly or collapse. A precaution Beyoncé followed while wearing stilettos in the movie *Dreamgirls* was to omit her famous booty-shaking move because the extreme tightness of Beyoncé's gowns threatened to tear a hole in the worst possible spot. "You can move it, but don't shake it," Robinson told Beyoncé.[6]

DANCING AROUND THE WORLD

When Beyoncé and Gaston selected 40 dancers for *The Beyoncé Experience Tour* in 2007, they taped more than 1,000 auditions to review later so they could be sure of their choices. A national organization representing the industry reported that hires for Beyoncé's 2007 videos received less than standard industry wages, although Beyoncé's staff justified the amount based on the elimination of the middleman and the direct dealings with the dancers. Industry experts, however, said that this nonstandard practice was "highly irregular" for someone with a high profile like Beyoncé.[7]

For most young dancers, though, pay is not the main event, as was the case of Kelly Spicer, from Arlington Heights, Illinois, who earned a place on Beyoncé's 2007 dance team. The dance teacher-turned pro said, "It's a dream come true."[8] Ashley Everett, from Chico, California, also won a spot on Beyoncé's international tour. Everett received the Most Well-Rounded Dancer award from San Jose's Urban Jamm Dance Convention and spent years dancing with the Chico Ballet and Full Force Hip-Hop & Jazz Co. in California before relocating to New York and graduating from the Professional Children's School. In October 2006, choreographer Frank Gatson invited Everett to audition for Beyoncé during a chance meeting at the Alvin Ailey School in New York. After asking her for a head shot and resumé, Gatson told her then to watch Beyoncé's rehearsal for the annual Fashion Rocks concert. In January 2007, Everett decided to audition, but first she had to stand outside in the freezing cold NYC weather with about 3,500 other dancers. After three hours, Everett's turn arrived and, luckily, Gatson remembered her. He asked her and three other girls to stay and learn the choreography for Beyoncé's "Déjà vu" track. After Gatson hired Everett for the 2007 tour, she flew to Los Angeles for 10 days to learn and rehearse the choreography from several Beyoncé videos. She wound up in two new videos. When the 2007 national tour opened in Tokyo before 40,000 people, technical problems dominated the evening. "It was a hot mess," Everett said. "It probably didn't look like it, but the

props, the costumes, the music, everything got messed up."[9] Beyoncé sang
a cappella at one point, and the dancers did without music.

BUZZIN' BEHIND THE QUEEN B

During *The Beyoncé Experience Tour* (2007), a 10-piece, all-girl band accompanied Beyoncé, as well as three vocalists: Tiffany Riddick, Montina
Cooper, and Crystal Collins. Calling themselves the Mamas and dressed
in 1960s style, the trio related to each other like sisters. The Mamas arranged the National Anthem for Destiny's Child, which the group performed at the 2006 NBA All Star Game, and toured with Mary J. Blige
and Jamie Foxx, but Collins and Riddick also perform solo. Collins, who
opened for national artists Gato Barbieri and Stanley Clarke, used to
travel abroad for the U.S. Department of Defense, entertaining military
troops and their families, and Riddick's credits include engagements with
Mariah Carey and Christina Aguilera.

Riddick was surprised to land the Beyoncé gig in 2007 because two
years earlier, Beyoncé's creative director wrote Riddick's name and phone
number down on what looked like a bubble gum wrapper. But the director
kept the wrapper all that time and when the tour was hiring, he surprised
Riddick by offering her a backup position. Riddick accepted because it
was a good fit and knew Beyoncé maintained a rigorous work schedule,
which appealed to her. Also, she felt she complemented Beyoncé's personality and vocal qualities, especially in tone and texture, and possessed
the flexibility to adapt to varying tempos. An added plus was that her
solo experience did not intimidate Beyoncé, who regularly introduces her
backup singers to audiences. "But you have to know the role you play,"
Riddick said.[10]

DRAMA COACH

Russian acting coach Ivana Chubbuck, in Los Angeles, assisted Beyoncé on at least two films: *Dreamgirls* and *Cadillac Records*. While preparing Beyoncé for the role of Deena in *Dreamgirls*, Chubbuck asked her pupil
to think of the song "Listen," which she would perform as a monologue,
and in which the character endeavors to empower herself as a woman,
liberating herself from the control of her manager-husband. Chubbuck
never allowed Beyoncé to sing the composition completely during rehearsals, because Chubbuck wanted the superstar to deliver the message
with the urgency and strength of someone whose emotional survival de-
pended on these qualities. Beyoncé could identify with this human need,

which helped her understand Deena's desperation. But in Beyoncé's next film—*Cadillac Records*—Chubbuck coached her using a different strategy. Since Beyoncé's character was based on heroin addict and singer Etta James, Chubbuck put Beyoncé through an exercise that makes a person feel stoned. "Not only did I feel organically high," Beyoncé said, "but it brought up emotions that made sense to someone who needed to take a drug such as this . . . to eliminate emotional pain."[11]

VOCAL COACHES

Another former Destiny's Child support person was Tennessee-based Kim Woods Sandusky, who also coached Pam Tillis, En Vogue, and various lesser-known R&B, pop, and country singers. Sandusky knows how to get the desired results from Beyoncé and taught her better breath control, as well as increased her vocal range so she could reach high notes more easily. David Brewer also contributed to Destiny's Child's and Beyoncé's career success. An international opera singer, Brewer, who coached Dawn Robinson (formerly of En Vogue), has a motto to the effect that every person has a unique voice that shows potential, but vocal development is a function of various different factors.

THE PRODUCERS

Record producers are ancillary personnel responsible for functions such as budgeting; supervising the recording, mixing, the mastering process, and coaching and guiding the musicians. Like movie directors, producers mold musical selections according to a vision and although Beyoncé produced many of her own tracks, she sometimes solicited help from other producers, among them Jermaine Dupri, Wyclef Jean, Dwayne Wiggins (of Tony! Toni! Tone), Rodney Jerkins, and She'kspre Briggs. Despite Destiny's Child's youth, Wiggins got involved because he knew the group was extremely focused. Another producer, Dan Workman from Beyoncé's hometown, collaborated with her on *Dangerously in Love*. Based at his renowned Sugar Hill Studio in Houston, Workman also produced records for other famous singers such as ZZ Top, Lyle Lovett, and Enrique Iglesias.

STRIKE UP THE BAND

After Beyoncé decided to hire an all-female band for *The Beyoncé Experience Tour* in 2007, she held open auditions at sites around the country. Before she was done, she had listened to hundreds of saxophonists, drum and keyboard players, percussionists, guitarists, and trumpet and bass instrumentalists. Bibi McGill, who has played guitar since she was 12 years old, auditioned in Los Angeles a few weeks before the tour started. But for final auditions, scheduled only days after her first audition, McGill was asked to fly to New York. Her plane got rerouted and she arrived six hours late, so McGill figured she was eliminated from the running, but she was wrong. "I played for about 20 seconds and everybody started screaming and basically I got the job on the spot," McGill said.[12] Until that moment, no guitarist had succeeded in meeting Beyoncé's standards, and ironically, McGill did not see Beyoncé until the next day. (Mathew auditioned and hired her.)

Actually, McGill and Beyoncé met in 2004 when McGill had been rehearsing for another gig and a girl walked by the door, backed up, hesitated, and then approached McGill, who assumed the visitor was an autograph seeker. "She comes up to me and says, 'Hi, you're the guitar player from Pink, huh'? I'm like, yeah, what's your name? She says, Beyoncé and I'm like, oh my god!"[13] McGill loved traveling and living the good life while on the Beyoncé 2007 tour, especially meeting fans. "Not a lot of people get to do what I do so I'm very thankful," she said.[14] Other band members felt the same way, such as bass guitar player Debbie Walker (aka "Divinity"), who first appeared with Beyoncé at the nationally televised BET awards in June 2006. Tia Fuller, an alto saxophonist and band leader from Aurora, Colorado, who called Beyoncé a workaholic, learned a lot about clarifying the vision of a musical piece. By the end of the tour, she was able to apply the technique to her specialty, which was jazz. She and the other band members, singers and dancers also learned a lot about Sasha, Beyoncé's energetic alter ego and the subject of the next chapter.

NOTES

1. Quoted in www.aris-dance.com.

2. Quoted by Mary Jane Mayturn, "The Graduates: Performing Arts Students Leave Louisville to Tackle the World of Entertainment," *Business First of Louisville*, July 24, 2006, www.newsbank.com (accessed June 6, 2008).

3. Quoted by Barbi Leifert, "Aspiring Dancers Leap at Chance to Showcase Work," *The Seattle Times*, July 5, 2007, www.newsbank.com (accessed June 6, 2008).

4. Quoted in "Beyoncé Knowles Says 'Crazy in Love' Was Love at First Listen," June 11, 2003, //music.yahoo.com (accessed June 6, 2008).

5. Quoted by Corey Moss, "Beyoncé Smitten by Triplets, Hungry Unknowns at Dance Audition," May 7, 2003, www.mtv.com (accessed June 6, 2008).

6. Quoted in "Bootylicious Beyoncé's Booty Shaking Ban!" *The Hindustan Times*, March 4, 2006, www.hindustan.com (accessed June 6, 2008).

7. Quoted in "Dancing for Beyoncé Is No Dream, Girl," www.TMZ.com (accessed June 6, 2008).

8. Quoted by Eileen O. Daday, "It's No Dream, Woman to Dance in Beyoncé Tour," *Daily Herald*, March 7, 2007, www.highbeam.com (accessed June 6, 2008).

9. Quoted by Christine G. K. La Pado, "Destiny's Other Child," *Chico News & Review*, November 15, 2007, www.newsbank.com (accessed June 6, 2008).

10. Ibid.

11. Quoted on www.ivanachubbuck.com (accessed January 17, 2009).

12. Quoted by Adeeba Folami, "Lady Guitarist Lives Her Musical Dreams," *The Black House News (BHN)*, September 13, 2007, www.newsbank.com (accessed June 6, 2008).

13. Ibid.

14. Ibid.

Chapter 11

SASHA AND SPIRITUALITY

"I guess when people talk about religion they think about nuns," Beyoncé said.[1] The word *religion* has many connotations, but most people agree that reverence toward a deity or Supreme Being is within the scope of the definition, as are attendance at a church, temple, or other gathering place; the knowledge and practice of certain rituals, liturgies, and customs; adherence to an ethical and moral code prohibiting heinous crimes such as murder, adultery, stealing, and other sins of commission and omission; and a respect for individual rights and property.

Nowhere in the definition of "religion," however, is there a green light for sexual license, which is at the core of Beyoncé's performance art. Regardless, the young diva maintains she can be both "bootylicious" and religious at the same time: "It's possible to believe in God and live your life right and still be sexy,"[2] says Beyoncé. One writer said Destiny's Child reflected the confused sexual attitude of the post-AIDS era, when the group married a "virginal sexual ethic with an up-front and frank sexual posturing"[3] and the Christian Worldview organization said Beyoncé's recycling of the whore-Madonna paradigm parallels Christians' spiritual dichotomy because Christians separate entertainment, politics, and science from their beliefs, permitting themselves to pay lip service to religious tenets even while buying tickets to the latest R-rated movie.[4]

THE INVENTION OF SASHA

Beyoncé admits she depends on her alter ego, Sasha, when appearing onstage or before a camera; and over the course of her career, Beyoncé and

Sasha have developed into two distinct sides of the same coin. As a child, Beyoncé first summoned Sasha as a crutch or aid to help her develop and capitalize on her talents. Indoctrinated into the Methodist religion and its attendant middle-class values, Beyoncé easily claimed the role of suburban school achiever. If not for her innate musical talents, Beyoncé might have progressed through her adolescence as just another attractive, intelligent young woman planning to attend college and pursue a career in social work or a similar field. But Beyoncé loved to sing, and as she honed her craft, she freed herself from some of the sociocultural constraints that deterred and unnerved her and caused anxieties that made her occasionally forget song lyrics or worry too much about who was or was not in the audience. Enter Sasha—the invention of a creative youngster timid about appearing in front of people and unleashing some of the inhibitions that kept her marching in a straight line. Sasha never felt self-conscious or inept; Sasha knew how to flaunt without offending and Sasha asserted herself without apology. As a result, Sasha helped a beguiling, musically precocious child morph into a dynamic entertainer. Beyoncé insists repeatedly that she's not Sasha, who is too flirtatious, super confident, fearless, aggressive, strong, sassy, and sexy for her own good.[5] The reason, she explains, is "I created my stage persona to protect myself."[6]

Unfortunately, however, Sasha confuses people, primarily fans, media people and others who cannot reconcile Beyoncé's stage persona with the devout Christian and spiritual person she professes to be. For instance in 2001, Beyoncé flew to Calgary in Canada, and, aligning herself with an educational group called Mad Moms against Bad Sex Ed, warned Canadian girls about the dangers of unplanned pregnancy. Beyoncé and other female celebrities espoused the message that if teens want to sleep around, they need to evaluate the options and take measures to prevent unwanted babies.[7] It is doubtful that Beyoncé's fellow church members would approve of the Houston star's "no, no, no" stance on abstinence, but undoubtedly Sasha approved.

Even Beyoncé seems awed and overwhelmed by this formidable, fun-loving, and feisty personality whom she claims is similar to a dramatic role, much like Foxxy Cleopatra in an *Austin Powers* flick. But a psychologist probably would declare Sasha a garden-variety defense mechanism—a way of neatening up Beyoncé's life so the good girl and the goddess can coexist in parallel universes. As far back as 2000, Beyoncé had a firm grasp on the Destiny's Child image. It was sexy and youthful—in a different way. That "way" included setting lively trends in fashion and bringing glamour back to R&B.

SPIRITUAL RETURNS

As a treatment against depression, the free-spirited, audacious Sasha succeeds to a greater extent than the introspective Beyoncé, but Sasha ultimately failed to rescue Beyoncé after her partners LaTavia and LeToya split from Destiny's Child. For several weeks, Beyoncé became severely introverted and unable to function, and nothing seemed to lift her spirits except attendance at church and conversations with God. Beyoncé believes the church keeps her sane and helps her combat negativity. She was comforted when her church congregation prayed for her and Destiny's Child when she went to church to relieve stress. Beyoncé believes faith in God enabled her and her family to cope with the law suits filed after the breakup of Destiny's Child. It also helped her survive many other rough times, such as her parents' six-month separation with its accompanying reduced income. "I know that God is a part of all of our lives," she said.[8]

Beyoncé received so much spiritual and emotional support from her family and church that it was easy to see why loyalty to this particular congregation precluded attendance at any other spiritual or secular institution. Beyoncé's parents derived much spiritual knowledge from the ministries of Pastors Rudy and Juanita Rasmus at St. John's United Methodist Church—so much, in fact, that they wanted to reward the church for its support. So in 2007, the Knowles family contributed $1 million to build a transitional living facility for the homeless,[9] a project that celebrated 16 years of the church's ministry to homeless and urban communities.

Beyoncé's sometimes submissive behavior can be partially attributed to her birth position in the family, as well as to her easy-going temperament, healthy acceptance of people, and inclination to act in a nonjudgmental way. For her, religion enhanced her acceptance of all people, particularly of gay men and women. To prove this to her fans, she allowed herself to be interviewed and photographed for the cover of *Instinct*, a national gay and lesbian publication. Her love and acceptance also encompassed a favorite uncle who died from AIDS. Her nonjudgmental attitude is attributed more to a respect for faith and spirituality than to established religion. She pledged to help others afflicted with AIDS, and this commitment applied to the hypothetical situation of Beyoncé parenting a gay son. She told *Instinct* that she would, of course, love this child in the same way she loved her gay fans.[10]

Beyoncé's sympathy for AIDS victims also translates to financial support. She raised money at an international AIDS benefit in South Africa, hosted by herself and Bono, in 2003, and, in early 2007, she appeared at

AmFAR's Gala in New York City, where she endorsed AmFAR's Campaign for AIDS research. In December 2007, Beyoncé and Kelly donated more than $250,000 to their Houston church's outreach project, a free temporary or long-term housing unit for persons with HIV/AIDS, the homeless, the developmentally disabled, and other at-risk families and individuals.

THE SECULAR CHURCH

Beyoncé first encountered the heavy influence of religion while growing up in the 1980s, when churches believed contemporary gospel music was a good tool for evangelizing communities. Beyoncé participated in the choir, probably learning as much from the choir director about capturing an audience's attention as she later absorbed from the videos of pop music icons. Her black, middle-class parents, like so many African American suburbanites in the 1980s, attained economic success, yet black researchers report that communities also needed a stabilizing force.[11] As a result, musicians incorporated more contemporary musical styles such as R&B, rap, and hip-hop into traditional gospel, thus secularizing the black church and simultaneously blurring the boundaries between spirituality and sexuality. Beyoncé could not avoid transferring her love and appreciation for gospel music into the secular sphere as a result of the gradual hybridization of the two.

When Beyoncé became a pop singer, she frequently returned to church to gather strength, demonstrating to herself and her audience that her Christian values inform her daily life and led her to disallow smoking, drinking, and swearing. The constant overlapping of her two worlds was mirrored in her role as the jazz-club-singer-cum-gospel-choir-member in *The Fighting Temptations*, a dramatic opportunity that must have seemed like a divinely inspired gift.

BODY AS A SACRED (OR SEXY?) VESSEL

Beyoncé's sexy moves onstage do not leave much to the imagination, but, according to her, "God wants people to celebrate their bodies—as long as you don't compromise your Christianity in the process."[12] Whether Beyoncé compromises her faith is strictly a matter of opinion. When Beyoncé performed with Destiny's Child, her movements communicated a savvy attitude and personal power (despite her feminized beauty) as she belted out her individuality and strength. But later on, as a solo act, she replaced the "independent women" or "survivor" with its polar opposite: the passive, male-dominated female sex object. Although Beyoncé never tried to pass herself off as an innocent schoolgirl, she progressively became "racier, edgier and with super sexualization,"[13] her music embracing male chauvinist pigs and macho-military-felon boyfriends.

Men have not missed Beyoncé's metamorphosis from ingénue to femme fatale, and officially she is the hottest woman alive, at least according to a 2007 Internet poll on Askmen.com.[14] Among 8.5 million voters, men cast Beyoncé as the Number 1 fantasy girlfriend, beating out actresses Scarlet Johansson and Jessica Alba and supermodel Adriana Lima. Add to that the provocative House of Dereon ad in which Beyoncé wore tight jeans and nothing else, and it's no wonder an anonymous fan summed up Beyoncé's message as "Dress like me and guys will love you."

Another example of Beyoncé's desire to cultivate a sexualized image is the cover of the booklet accompanying her CD, *B'Day*. Wearing black heels and a swimsuit and trailing two alligators on leashes, "Sasha" stares back at fans. Think dominatrix and you would not be wrong, a black UCLA professor opined. She believes Beyoncé projects the image of a "she-devil" who defines "her self-worth by how much of her body she can show."[15] For further proof, look at her steamy cover photo in the 2007 *Sports Illustrated Swimsuit Issue*. It shows a smiling Beyoncé bedecked in a bikini (not by accident is it designed by the House of Dereon). In interviews Beyoncé flaunts the cover as a singular accomplishment: the first musician and only the second black woman to grace the cover.

In actuality, the other Beyoncé—the one who swears she is really nothing at all like the vixen Sasha—stands in silent awe of her curvaceous counterpart. To the question, do you see any conflict between being religious and cultivating a sexy image? Beyoncé answered: "No. What's more important is how I treat people and what I give them."[16] Beyoncé is so used to the blending of sex and spirituality that when she returns to Houston, she still feels like that good-old country girl who likes fried chicken and going barefoot.

She is also a woman who projects herself as a good role model who knows how to show her gratefulness for her good fortune. During an acceptance speech in 2003, when she won four awards from *Billboard Magazine*, she thanked God for the opportunities He made possible. But not everyone admires Beyoncé for her deference to religion; for instance, the founder of The Body Shop, Dame Anita Roddick, berated Beyoncé and other pop icons, calling them part of the pimp and whore culture that pays homage to the sex industry.[17]

THE ETHICS OF SEX

Regardless of the reasons, the morality police have spoken. In 2006, the National Organization for Women condemned Beyoncé's and any other female celebrity's perpetuation of stereotyped and sexualized behavior. The group's stance originated from a survey in which 82 percent of mothers regarded celebrity behaviors as the Number 1 media-associated challenge to parenting children. The American Psychological Association also issued a statement criticizing the portrayal of women as sex objects, emphasizing the negative effect on women's self-images.

Several years later, it does not look like Beyoncé has heard the message, as two music videos produced from Beyoncé's *B'Day* CD weighed in as highly sexualized. Her signature dance helped Beyoncé win an MTV Video Music Award in 2003 for best R&B video and best choreographer—validation that at least the industry approves of the graphic use of sex. And the debate rages on. One music critic said, "Sexual power can be powerful, but with Beyoncé . . ., there is no mystery. Everything is displayed like a buffet, leaving no room for future growth or artistic evolution."[18] On the other hand, another critic called Beyoncé "pretty," "clean," and a "vavoomish ambassador for pop music."[19]

HIP OR HYPOCRITICAL?

If sex and violence have insinuated their all-pervasive way into the music industry, is Beyoncé hip or hypocritical? Many argue that one woman alone cannot resist the collective responses of song writers and the merchandisers and marketers of pop music, who encourage physical lewdness, misogyny, and other political incorrectness. As such, Beyoncé's responsibility should be limited only to the songs she composes. The Christian group United by One believes entertainers have a limited responsibility; it exhorts people not to compare Christians to a model of perfection, because compromising one's faith may be a by-product of conforming to industry standards. United by One takes the position that Christian entertainers need prayers and support, not harsh words or reprisals, and people need to highlight the positive aspects of Christian celebrities in order to increase spiritual relationships. Thus when Beyoncé and other musicians refer to God in award acceptance speeches, it is perceived as nonobjectionable behavior. Too many nonbelievers like to emphasize religious hypocrisy, using the slightest deviation—a thank-you speech, interview, or even a record label association—to indict the celebrity when what people really need to do is permit Christians to have their flaws.[20]

NAUGHTY GIRL

Although religious practitioners often prefer not "to cast the first stone," feminists do not hesitate to throw a punch or two, deploring Beyoncé's gradual segue to the sexual side of the street, as seen in her album *Dangerously in Love*. In the track "Naughty Girl" she initiates a sexual rendezvous, and although it is role reversal, the male is still a sex object, and rationalizing it as payback still dehumanizes and objectifies the person. The prurient material in *B'Day* also incensed feminists writing for *MP: A Feminist Journal Online*, although Beyoncé's philosophy is far from clear-cut and well defined.[21] Beyoncé's "Irreplaceable," which argues for the elimination of hurtful men from women's lives, can inspire confidence in females who hold feminist values of self-empowerment and autonomy, but on the other hand, Beyoncé and her rapper-husband Jay-Z can perpetuate hip-hop's obsession with a Bonnie and Clyde relationship. Many feminists have argued that hip-hop demonizes black female sexuality with its use of terms such as "bitches" and "hoes" for women and the gravitation toward "Jezebel" figures and homophobia themes. For black feminist bell hooks, gangsta rap also qualifies as antifeminist, with Jay-Z representing the quintessential player in this scenario and Beyoncé his "silent, willing stripper."[22] Other experts look toward more generalized areas than Beyoncé to affix blame. For example, Russell Simmons, cofounder of Def Jam Records and a pioneering hip-hop producer, and African American documentary filmmaker Byron Hurt believe music profiteers catering to a sexist society will sell anything hot and in demand (and not necessarily socially redeeming) and must accept some of the blame because artists then respond to basic supply-and-demand economics.

I AM . . . SASHA FIERCE

In November 2008, Beyoncé responded to the market's relentless demand for the vocal talents of her alter ego by dedicating her new double album, *I Am . . . Sasha Fierce*, to her fiery counterpart. A month previously, Beyoncé released two singles from the double album—"If I Were a Boy" from *I Am* and "Single Ladies (Put a Ring on It)" from *Sasha Fierce*. She explained that half the record exposes the real, more introspective Beyoncé "underneath all the makeup, underneath the lights"; the other half showcases Sasha Fierce. Beyoncé acknowledges that it's risky revealing the true Beyoncé through songs such as "Broken Hearted Girl" and "Halo," but Sasha balances those glimpses into the authentic Beyoncé with more gutsy, fun numbers such as "Diva" and "Sweet Dreams."[23] The latter allow her to "really step out of myself," she says.[24]

By the beginning of 2009, *I Am . . . Sasha Fierce* made *Billboard Magazine*'s Top 10 albums, and two of the tracks—"If I Were a Boy" and "Single Ladies (Put a Ring on It)"—hit the Top 10 chart and were drawing record Internet crowds to YouTube.[25] It appeared that Sasha could do no wrong.

NOTES

1. Quoted by Amy Reiter, "Backstreet's Carter Wailed throughout Arrest—Juicy Bits," January 8, 2002, www.Salon.com (accessed June 14, 2008).

2. Ibid.

3. Valerie Lowe, "Living Pure in an R-Rated Culture," *Charisma*, February 2006, www.charismamag.com (accessed September 6, 2008).

4. Quoted by Lowe.

5. Quoted by Associated Press, "Beyoncé Transforms into 'Sasha' Onstage," *China Daily*, December 16, 2006, www.chinadaily.com (accessed May 8, 2008).

6. Ibid.

7. Quoted by Carmen Wittmeier, "Mad Moms Against Chastity," *Alberta Report*, June 25, 2001, www.findarticles.com (accessed May 29, 2008).

8. Quoted by Beyoncé Knowles, Kelly Rowland, and Michelle Williams, *Soul Survivors: The Official Autobiography of Destiny's Child* (New York: Regan Books, 2002), 75.

9. "Beyoncé, Tina, Mathew, Kelly and the Survivor Foundation . . .," *Market Wire*, September 11, 2007, www.marketwire.com (accessed September 7, 2008).

10. Quoted in Mike Wood, "Beyoncé: Destiny Calls Again," *Instinct Magazine*, December 1, 2006, www.instinctmagazine.com (accessed May 8, 2008).

11. Quoted by Melinda E. Weekes, "This House, This Music: Exploring the Interdependent Interpretive Relationship Between the Contemporary Black Church and Contemporary Gospel Music," *Black Music Research Journal*, March 22, 2005, www.highbeam.com (accessed May 8, 2008).

12. Quoted in "Gospel Singer," www.hellomagazine.com/jmusic/specials/beyoncé (accessed May 8, 2008).

13. Quoted by Natalie Y. Moore, "Beyoncé's Bootyful B'Day," *In These Times*, www.inthesetimes.com (accessed May 8, 2008).

14. "Survey of Fantasy Girlfriend," 2007, www.askmen.com (accessed September 7, 2008).

15. Quoted by Gail Wyatt, "PBS Transcript of Travis Smiley Interview with Wyatt. Special Feature: Road to Health," March 31, 2005, www.pbs.org (accessed May 8, 2008).

16. Quoted by Lisa Robinson, "Above and Beyoncé," *Vanity Fair*, November 2005, www.accessmylibrary.com (accessed September 7, 2008).

17. Laura Smith, "Beyoncé @Pimp Culture Blast," February 21, 2006, www.thisislongon.co.uk (accessed May 8, 2008).

18. Quoted by Moore.

19. Quoted by Sean Daly, "And the Grammys Will Go to . . .," February 7, 2008, www.blogs.tampabay.com/popmusic (accessed May 5, 2008).

SASHA AND SPIRITUALITY

111

20. Quoted by Kimberley, "Famous, Successful and Christian?" www.united-byone.co.uk (accessed May 8, 2008).

21. Faedra Chatard Carpenter, "An Interview with Gwendolyn D. Pough," *Callaloo*, 2006, //muse.jhu.edu (accessed May 8, 2008).

22. Quoted by Nghana Lewis, "You Sell Your Soul Like You Sell a Piece of Ass. . .," *Black Music Research Journal*, March 22, 2005, www.highbeam.com (accessed May 8, 2008).

23. "Beyoncé Reveals Title and Details About Her Forthcoming Double Album 'I Am . . . Sasha Fierce' Available Everywhere Tuesday, November 18," *PR Newswire*, October 22, 2008, www.highbeam.com (accessed October 4, 2009).

24. Ibid.

25. The Associated Press, "Top Songs," *Telegraph-Herald* (Dubuque), December 21, 2008, www.highbeam.com (accessed January 17, 2009).

Chapter 12

THE BEYONCÉ EXPERIENCE

The thoughts, ideas, and actions of the rich and famous generally carry greater weight than those of neighbors, friends, or acquaintances. This is the paradox of the twenty-first century: Those furthest removed from the masses often influence the most. Beyoncé is no exception; with a bat of her eyelashes, the pop singer can initiate changes in consumers' responses to politics, fashion, advertising, social mores, and much more. To many of her fans, especially teens and young adults, her support for an issue is like *Good Housekeeping's* stamp of approval, and a thumbs-down might mean the difference between a teen staying in school or dropping out.

Maureen Orth, author of *The Importance of Being Famous*, believes media coverage has changed from public knowledge of a celebrity's body of work, talent, skills, or performance to public knowledge of a celebrity's lifestyle and indiscretions, with the result that television shows like *Entertainment Tonight* get high ratings for reporting facts, as well as speculating on a celebrity's every word and action. One reason for this endless parade of sound and video bites is that famous people strive to stay in the limelight and preserve their image, a reality that may or may not be compromised or enhanced by their behaviors. This is why before interviews, entertainers often are prepared extensively by publicists, managers, or handlers. Reporters learn that certain questions are off limits or simply evaded by the celebrity under a pretense of ignorance. Sometimes celebrities such as Beyoncé avoid the physical proximity of fans and others by hiring bodyguards, who keep away undesirables who might wish to provoke altercations or solicit favors. And all of the hoopla surrounding the comings and goings of famous personages are covered not only by tabloid journalists, but even by mainstream publications like the *New York Times* and *Washington Post*.

UNDER THE INFLUENCE

So it is that readers and viewers wind up knowing little about the professional lives of celebrities and a great deal about their attitudes and influences. "They try to minimize their unguarded exposure and the stage to their advantage," wrote Orth.[1] Another name for this is branding, in which an orchestrated campaign is launched to build a performer's name, reputation, credibility, and image into a marketable, tangible asset. Managers, publicists, and promotional staff create brands, but so do specialized agencies and management firms recently propagated by this new industry. For example, hip-hop music eased into branding by means of high-profile personalities such as Eminem, Jay-Z, and Queen Latifah, and these stars profited financially from the heavy exposure. Several years ago Beyoncé joined the ranks of those whose unique brand permeates the lives of millions. At the same time and not so coincidentally, Beyoncé clammed up on the media. "Not speaking about your personal life controls your brand," she said in November 2008.[2] Celebrities, however, cannot control their brand 100 percent.

Every celebrity's brand is vulnerable to scandal as the Martha Stewarts, Britney Spears, and Kobe Bryants can attest to, although notoriety often materializes into only a temporary inconvenience in the right hands. When Oprah gave her blessings to a memoir writer later accused of falsifying portions of his writings, the taint of her misjudgment temporarily disturbed her image, but a heart-felt apology to her audience and a genuine verbal thrashing hurled at the errant author erased Oprah's "guilt by association," with the result that her audience of millions soon forgave her. Nothing sordid (except the Destiny's Child split) has touched Beyoncé thus far, but her marriage surely will affect perceptions of her brand and only time will tell whether it diminishes in power or gains strength. One clue to her future influence came in 2006 when Beyoncé and her then-beau, Jay-Z, were listed as a Power Couple on *Time Magazine*'s 100 Most Influential People list; in another decade, who knows how many illustrious titles the hip-hop king and the R&B queen may accumulate.

TOBACCO

As a Christian, Beyoncé does not drink, smoke, or swear, but she might just as well have, for in February 2007, ads came out showing her holding a cigarette. Critics castigated Beyoncé, complaining that her influence over teens—especially black girls—might lead to an increase in smoking among African Americans. Many detractors believed she was sexy with or without a cigarette, and since smoking was the Number 1 killer among African Americans (37% show difficulty in stopping), Beyoncé did not have to contribute to the high percentage by appearing in an ad with a cigarette.[3] The discrepancy between what Beyoncé said and what she did triggered the disfavor of antismoking groups in Ireland and Australia during *the 2007 Beyoncé Experience Tour.* The group Quit argued that the poster of Beyoncé communicated that smoking was chic, and the Queensland Cancer Fund concurred, adding that Beyoncé was so talented (she always sold out shows) that she did not also have to sell out to tobacco interests.

FOOD AND FITNESS

After that incident, Beyoncé's image makers made sure she stayed at least 100 miles from any cigarette, but food was another matter entirely. Judging by Beyoncé's admissions in her autobiography and to the press, she gravitated toward a low-fat, low-carb diet with occasional binges of junk food and deep fried chicken. "I would rather eat than go somewhere on vacation," Beyoncé confided to a reporter. "I'd rather eat than shop."[4] Beyoncé's predilection for fried foods, chocolate, and ice cream did not endear her to dietitians and nutrition purists, but her average dinner in 2004, baked chicken marinated with fresh garlic and seasoned with salt, black pepper, and Cayenne pepper, was lean enough to satisfy the average health-conscious consumer. Another eat-right strategy Beyoncé used was to reverse her food schedule and sit down to her biggest meal at breakfast; in the evenings, she ingested a bowl of granola or another favorite cereal.

Occasionally, Beyoncé wants to drop weight quickly and uses a lemon-water drink to cleanse her system,[5] at which point her critics accuse her of catering to the "you-can-never-be-too-thin" contingent. As a onetime spokesperson for Pepsi, Beyoncé, of course, washed everything down with the bubbly beverage or, during the Milk Campaign and the Mother-Daughter Role Modeling Summit held September 27, 2006, she kicked back a few glasses of the "perfect food" to remind her fans that milk was a sensible weight-maintenance beverage. In another interview, this time in 2007, Beyoncé said she drinks plenty of water, but no booze. "Alcohol will kill anything that's alive, and preserve anything that's dead," she said.[6]

Image makers have also used Beyoncé's naturally lush figure as a symbol of empowerment and independence because she outright rejected the skinny look, usually retaining a moderate amount of body fat. That physical standard plus regular exercise (such as twirling hula hoops, swimming, roller-skating, aerobic exercising, running 30 minutes every day, or completing as many sit-ups at night as she can) allows her to avoid a steady diet of carrot and celery sticks. As a result, Beyoncé's weight influence on teens and young women is mainly positive, as her body is more curvaceous than lithe. She sets a realistic goal for young Americans, who typically embrace the standard of thinness, especially those with eating disorders, while Russians and other cultures judge beautiful women in terms of femininity, intelligence, and manners. Some American women would give millions of dollars to look like Jennifer Aniston, but others mention the influence of more buxom models such as Jennifer Lopez and Beyoncé, who made it okay to be a black woman with heavier thighs, a smaller waist, and ample butt, although Beyoncé's "sincerity" image diminished a little when she appeared 20 pounds lighter for *Dreamgirls*.

POLITICS

Beyoncé, like most entrepreneurs, exhibits an abiding respect and affection for capitalism. In 1999, women owned nearly 40 percent of U.S. businesses, and many more operate in the corporate sector today, including celebrities like Oprah Winfrey, Debbi Fields, and Jenny Craig.[7] After seeing *The Beyoncé Experience* in 2007, national columnist Dr. Anthony Asadullah Samad, author of *Saving the Race: Empowerment Through Wisdom*, wrote that Beyoncé's all-female 10-piece band (named Suga Mama), along with her 3 backup singers, 10 dancers, and countless costume changes, hinted at what a matriarchy might resemble.[8] The move toward an all-women production was not accidental, for Beyoncé and her advisers strive to perpetuate an image or brand with which her fans can identify, although her brand of feminist politics is intentionally overlaid with sex. This is why male critics react positively to the entertainer, whom Samad called an "Amazon of massive proportions: beauty, talent and intelligence"[9] whose empowering music and lyrics rouse both old and young women to action, as is indicated in the "Irreplaceable" lyric, "To the left, to the left, everything you own in a box to the left."

Beyoncé piggybacks sex with feminism to the extent that she cancelled a performance in Malaysia because Muslim groups demanded a much tamer dress code for the cast of *The Beyoncé Experience* and Beyoncé refused to compromise. Ethiopia accepted her mini-skirt-navel-bearing costumes, however, and she celebrated that country's millennium with the blessing of the Ethiopian patriarch of the Orthodox Church. Beyoncé's image and feminist outlook dictate that she will not capitulate to any man who forces women to live under severe restrictions. Her political views also follow the black tradition of supporting the Hip-Hop Action Network's voter registration program, which encourages more progressive political attitudes. In March 2008, during the Democratic primary races, she supported Barack Obama (as opposed to Hillary Clinton), attending a $2,300-per person fundraiser in New York and indicating her preference to vote along racial, rather than gender, lines. Husband Jay-Z threw his support to Obama, too, because Jay-Z believes the Illinois senator—like Martin Luther King Jr.—could bring positive and peaceful change to the country and unite America's disenfranchised, especially children.

THE COLORS OF RACE

When Beyoncé appeared inside and on the cover of the 2007 Swimsuit Issue of *Sports Illustrated,* she was only the second black woman ever to do so. Similarly, when she won the ASCAP Songwriter of the Year Award in 2001, she was the first black woman to earn this honor. The attainment of these goals clearly demonstrates Beyoncé's influence on race, as she gave African Americans, especially females, another reason to be proud of their heritage. In a society in which black women face economic discrimination, Beyoncé beat the odds and showed white, Hispanic, and Asian groups that African Americans can reach for high goals, too. Academics noted and made much of this, concluding that Beyoncé and other celebrities of mixed race (e.g., J-Lo, Tiger Woods, and Christina Aguilera) opened doors for talented people as a result of these celebrities' "ethnically ambiguous" appearances. Ambiguity captivates consumers because it reflects a younger, multiracial segment of the general population. Although Beyoncé is portrayed as an innocent model of femininity, her fashion attire, jewelry, physical appearance, and even photographic poses emphasize the ethnic ambiguity of both black and white characteristics. For actors and models, ambiguity is desirable because of the potential for multiple remunerations from a wider range of work opportunities, so Beyoncé emphasizes her black and Creole-mixed heritage by tinting her locks blond. Fans with and without mixed heritage applaud her strength and decisiveness, but Beyoncé's racial ambiguity unwittingly exacerbates pressure on African American females already stigmatized by a black community that believes black is good (but lighter is better). Black law professor Kimberly Jade Norwood takes ambiguity a step further in explaining the different racial stereotypes (blackness means guns, violence, and failure; whiteness correlates with Harvard, CEO, and success) and how they generate stigmas. For example, a self-acknowledged "oreo" (defined as a person black on the outside and white on the inside), Norwood recalls how her smartness and ambition in high school were disdained by her black peers because of the "white" stigma attached to it.[10] Norwood's thesis raises the question, has Beyoncé's ambitious rise to stardom resulted from a racial ambiguity that went deeper than physical appearance?

Critics claim that Beyoncé has increased the use of skin lighteners among young urban-educated women in the global South. The practice is also fueled by print, Internet, and television ads to the tune of $95 million a year.[11] African American teens and young women buy bleaching products to attract black men beguiled by images in magazines such as *Ebony, Jet,* and *Essence,* which reinforce ambiguous cultural standards and lend credence to the rumors that Beyoncé bleaches her skin and/or magazines or companies like L'Oreal digitally alter the images. Beyoncé's racial influence does not stop with skin shade because in an effort to emulate Beyoncé, teens also straighten their hair or add European-style straight-hair extenders. Standards of beauty are so racially slanted toward white characteristics that when *Glamour Magazine* recently hosted a roundtable for African American women, their hair stories all screamed "white influence."[12] Dreads had been abandoned, hair was blown out, and Afros were relegated to the 1960s closet. When college professor Venus Opal Reese interviewed 200 black women in 2006 for her play *Split Ends* (about the history of black women's hair), she learned that the majority of criticism they received about their natural hair styles came from black people, and some black women even resorted to plastic surgery to narrow their noses. "We have a history of not being valued that we still impose on each other," Reese said. "I don't want to sound cavalier, but nobody's got a whip over our backs."[13]

To be fair, Beyoncé alone cannot be held responsible for perpetuating intraracial discrimination. A study of 2,700 advertisements in *Cosmopolitan* and *Essence* magazines between 1974 and 2003 found that whereas the number of ads featuring African American women increased in *Cosmopolitan*, the number in *Essence* decreased.[14] Results also indicated that the African American models in the ads were more likely to display European characteristics in skin tone, hair texture, body type, and eye color. Even Beyoncé felt pressured to straighten her hair in 2003, when she decided to go natural for a while. But some people called her hair style ugly and challenged her decision to the point that while walking through airport security dressed in a warm-up suit, tennis shoes, and hat, she was stopped by the baggage screener, who reprimanded her for not dressing and looking the way she did on TV.[15]

SCHOOL IS COOL!

Ambiguity also insinuated its way into Beyoncé's influence on education because she was home-schooled and tutored from eighth grade on and did not receive a conventional secondary school education. The Professional Association of Teachers—the union for education professionals in the United Kingdom—agrees that a better strategy would be to draft role models with jobs requiring intelligence rather than physical aesthetics. Educational leaders argue that too many of young people's idols (usually singers, actors, and sports personalities such as Sean Connery, Brazilian World Cup winner Ronaldo, and Keira Knightley) boast they did poorly in school but succeeded anyway. And teachers' perceptions of students change if they observe students falling under the influence of celebrities, according to the Centre for Public Policy Research at King's College in London, which conducted three studies of 14- to 16-year-old girls and found that many teens equated success with attaining an attractive and feminine appearance á la Beyoncé.[16] Teens who chose this route—even those classified as "good pupils"—were regarded with disdain by educators, who often punished the teens for wearing too much jewelry or what they deemed inappropriate clothing and makeup. Some of these working class and minority teens eventually dropped out of school and never attained success like their role models, because even their physical assets fell below current standards of beauty.

On the positive side, however, celebrities can influence students when, as noted by Barking Abbey School in the United Kingdom, a former pupil and singer/songwriter like Billy Bragg speaks to pupils and boosts the benefits of education. Also, school-linked programs involving celebrities can motivate teens, such as the 2007 Disney Dreamers Academy, which used interactive workshops and sports and entertainment celebrities such as R&B recording artist Musiq and Terrance J of BET's *106 & Park* to pique the interest of 100 U.S. secondary students in grades 9–12.[17] Disney also threw in a trip to Walt Disney World Resort in Florida that was hosted by radio personality Steve Harvey and included empowerment sessions. Another program, called Music Inspires Health and founded by Georgia medical school student Benjamin Levy, connected kids with musicians approved by an advisory board, and the musicians delivered health messages to teens, usually on a topic of special interest to the artists. Beyoncé has not participated directly or indirectly in any teen motivational program to stay in school and get a solid education, except for the funding of music education in Texas public schools and other states. Thus her influence on schooling remains, at best, neutral.

FOR THE SAKE OF FEMINISM

This does not hold true, however, for her role modeling of feminism because when African American teacher-writer Zetta Elliott, an avowed feminist, wrote about an after-school program for teen girls in the journal *Third Space*, she asked the girls for their role models and the teens cited Beyoncé, Aaliyah, and other celebrities. Elliott concluded that although black women such as Condoleeza Rice and Oprah have assumed prominent positions in society, the African American woman's status has not markedly improved because of pervasive myths and stereotypes, and she wondered if Beyoncé and other artists could transcend the combined pressures of race, gender, and sex.[18] Elliot would have felt more optimistic about the future of feminism among black teens if they had referenced black feminist scholars instead of celebrities. And U.S. teens are not the only ones reacting this way. Western influence has infiltrated the Mali female's mindset in Africa and changed her views on autonomy, sexuality, and gender role to the degree that on International Women's Day in 2006, teens in Mali (West Africa) opted for Beyoncé-style behavior and, accordingly, wore jeans and nail polish and discussed the size of their bust.

Academics like Samantha C. Thrift believe Beyoncé's influence on feminist attitudes is ambiguous at best, with Beyoncé's lyrics and images creating a third-wave feminism that, despite the singer's emphasis on economic empowerment, projects images of a sexualized feminine role in heterosexual relationships; thus the polarity of views ultimately confuses and demoralizes young women.[19] But Princeton University professor Daphne Brooks disagrees and points out that in Beyoncé's album *B'Day*, the singer alludes to women survivors of Hurricane Katrina and their attempts to transcend their despair and deal with the problems wrought by the catastrophe. Thus, she says, Beyoncé's music is a form of "protest singing," and instead of revisiting the angry black woman stereotype, the pop vocalist sent a message of political recovery—that black females could emerge from their grief, confront the devastation, and replace their prior possessions and relationships with new ones.[20]

COMMERCIALISM

Although Beyoncé appears to waffle in her attitudes about feminism, she is straightforward and direct in demonstrating her views on money. She wages a 365-day-a-year campaign to tap into the large amounts of disposable income of young adults. Her assimilated musical style (a combination of pop, R&B, soul, and hip-hop), an ambiguous ethnic appeal to a wide audience, and her racial identification now extend to the Latino community. In 2007, Beyoncé responded to this new population by reissuing *B'Day* with seven tracks in Spanish, including a duet with Shakira. The statistics of a growing global Hispanic market indicate increased revenues for Beyoncé and her brand, so she also recorded Spanish versions of hits such as "Irreplaceable" and "Listen" from the film *Dreamgirls*, as well as a duet with Mexico's Alejandro Fernandez for a telenovela version of *Zorro*. That move propelled her onto *People en Espanol*'s "50 Most Beautiful List," where she was the sole Latina.

What's more, Beyoncé turns in performances that resonate with dance fans and those enamored of spectacles, empowered and/or sexy women, and the famous trademark "butt role" or hip thrust movement. Beyoncé exhilarates audiences by singing along with the backing track during live performances and throwing in melismata (singing several different notes on one syllable). And when it comes to eye-catching effects, no one delivers better ones than Beyoncé, who borrowed the techniques from Madonna and Michael Jackson. Beyoncé makes dramatic stage entrances such as being lowered from the rafters by a rope; and in the style of female pop music stars Mariah Carey, Britney Spears, and Jennifer Lopez, Beyoncé uses high-tech stage equipment and music videos to market her talents, make shows memorable, and keep her fans happily opening their billfolds.

Even when the digital technology fails, Beyoncé wins, as seen when one of the lighting effects malfunctioned at the start of a performance of *The Beyoncé Experience* in St. Louis. Beyoncé appeared on stage surrounded by a blaze of pyrotechnics, but one of the fireworks bounced off stage and into the first row. Two young people were later treated for minor burns at the hospital, and Beyoncé visited them after the performance and apologized profusely. The accident and the attendant hospital visit attracted media attention.

Other good news for Beyoncé is that although special effects cost big bucks, ticket holders—not entertainers—usually end up bearing their costs. The result is that concert prices in the 1990s hit new highs, mainly because of special effects, but singers and their entourages still take home a bundle of cash. According to Princeton University, performers earn most of their incomes from concert revenues and, depending on the performer's draw, the ticket prices—and thus the net profits—vary. For instance, in April 2004, Beyoncé, Alicia Keys, Missy Eliott, and Tamia performed at

Madison Square Garden in New York City and ticket prices averaged $81 for their show, but a month later, Yes performed there and ticket prices averaged $61.[21]

Endorsement deals also rake in the big bucks, and publicists and advertisers often brag they can take an unknown artist and make that person into an icon with a brand value sold to diverse markets. A branded celebrity's personality values can be auctioned to the highest bidder, or the celebrity can represent a preexisting value package that has market appeal. For instance, Pepsi's pre-Athens 2004 Olympics advertising campaign brought together Britney Spears, Beyoncé, Pink, Enrique Iglesis, and members of Queen in a female gladiator commercial in which the performers sang "We Will Rock You," which supposedly communicated that although the entertainers were rivals, Pepsi drinkers had a kinship that transcended the competition. It is hype and hokum, but hype and hokum that sold well, and Beyoncé used her brand for a million-dollar ride.[22]

To maximize sales, however, celebrities and products must complement each other. Market researchers emphasize criteria such as physical attractiveness and credibility to help make a good fit. Another important factor is similarity between the celebrity's image and the consumers' attitudes regarding the printed ads and the brand. Florida State University consumer science student Karla Renton researched the correlation between the likeability and attractiveness of a celebrity and consumers' positive attitudes toward the ad and the product. She found that the celebrity's popularity among consumers and the media ultimately affected how people viewed them in the advertisement. Beyoncé's brand as a "good girl" who happens to be gorgeous increases her desirability as a product endorser. Because commercials and advertisements are repeated endlessly in magazines and newspapers and on radio, television, and the Internet, the total effect can trigger one of two negative consumer reactions. Either consumers morph into shopaholics, as reported by the National Consumer Council in London, or they become cynics, desensitized and mistrustful of the motives of the endorsers.[23] In short, females easily lose faith in products, and this is exacerbated when, as in Beyoncé's case, her face becomes ubiquitous. Overexposure can ruin a good celebrity-endorser because teens can start exhibiting skepticism over the product, hypothesizing, for example, that the "improved look" is more a function of the photographer's airbrushing then the intrinsic worth of the product.

Beyoncé and her handlers guard her image carefully because they know it is synonymous with cash. As one of the priciest "symbols of Hollywood commerce,"[24] Beyoncé's brand can be compromised by almost anything—

any imperfection or defect. For example, when she fell down a flight of stairs at a July 2007 concert in Orlando, Florida, Beyoncé did not immediately worry about injuries nor did she appear embarrassed. What bothered her most was thousands of people clicking on the YouTube video replay of the incident because she feared it might compromise her "brand identity." For celebrities, these can be deal-breaking concerns, and the way Beyoncé manages these kinds of threats shows she still is a woman of influence when it comes to marketing wizardry—it has made her a wealthy woman, and, although people taunt her about her numerous endorsements and potential for overexposure, others respect her for her money-making moxie.

FASHION

As the House of Dereon's celebrity figurehead, Beyoncé alerts consumers to what is trendy and cool. Beyoncé's shape approximates the weight and dimensions of real women—white and black—so her clothing line or brand claims a special niche in the market. The clothes sell for higher prices and target a wider range of ages, and many females covet couture advice from Beyoncé and other celebrity-designer competitors such as Gwen Stefani, Madonna, Avril Lavigne, and J-Lo. Teens generate a majority of the buying power for House of Dereon. "My big fashion influences are my family, Beyoncé, and Kimora Lee Simmons," said Alexis Anderson, a 17-year-old dancer from Corpus Christi, Texas.[25]

House of Dereon was a natural outgrowth of Destiny's Child's designs for performances and professional appearances. Tina practiced her craft, creating different fashions cut from the same materials and tailored into such separates as hot pants, cropped tops, black leather pants, halters, and mix-and-match crystal-studded bras. For the 2005 Grammys, for instance, each member of Destiny's Child modeled a different version of a green-sequined cutaway gown. Today, Beyoncé advises Tina about the fashion designs because she knows what to look for in well-fitted clothes and can contribute creative ideas based on her travels and activities, as well as on sketches and the vintage items she spots in antique stores.

MUSIC TO THEIR EARS

That Beyoncé influenced and will continue to influence the music industry, especially R&B, is a foregone conclusion, and many music critics have remarked on her performance contributions (see appendix on Album Reviews). At this writing Beyoncé's recent album, *B'Day*, received a mixed review from *The New Yorker*, which noted that although Beyoncé's voice is still great, she strained more than once and deteriorated into shouts.[26] Included on the album is the hit single "Irreplaceable," which was not originally written for Beyoncé (or any woman, for that matter), but rather for the country-western category. American R&B pop singer/songwriter Ne-Yo wrote the lyrics for a man, but then decided the words were more empowering for women and Beyoncé wanted to record an honest track that women could relate to. She changed the arrangement somewhat, adding drums and transposing it to a higher key, but the content remained the same and made the track an instant hit. In fact, some critics believe "Irreplaceable" is the best track on *B'Day* because of its strong stance on undeserving men. When Beyoncé was interviewed on Larry King's show, she said, "We (women) can't forget our power and our worth."[27]

WHAT'S AHEAD

With Beyoncé on the minds and lips of thousands of teens and young adults each day, as they buy CDs and clothes, watch videos on TV, view *Dreamgirls*, or contribute to a charity the entertainer supports, it is not hard to understand why the famous singer-actress-model-record producer-entrepreneur-philanthropist might find it hard to be humble. Few people have the honor of performing "The Way We Were" for legendary songstress Barbra Streisand at a Kennedy Center tribute, *and*, in the same month (January 2009), serenading the newly inaugurated President Barack Obama and his First Lady with the standard ballad "At Last." But foretelling how Beyoncé will treat her far-reaching success is surely not a task for the fainthearted.

What's even harder is predicting her contributions in the performing arts, and perhaps in other fields, over the next 25 to 50 years. But whatever Beyoncé determines her destiny to be, you can bet that the mild-mannered Texas troubadour will endeavor to make it come true.

NOTES

1. Maureen Orth, *The Importance of Being Famous: Behind the Scenes of the Celebrity-Industrial Complex* (New York: Henry Holt, 2004), 19.

2. Jeannine Amber, "I Am Legend," *Essence*, November 2008, www.web.ebscohost.com (accessed November 2, 2008).

3. Dave Newhouse, "Berkley Activist Awarded for War on Smoking," *Oakland Tribune*, April 30, 2007, //findarticles.com (accessed September 12, 2008).

4. Quoted by Max Vadukul, "Queen B," *Independent on Sunday*, September 3, 2006, www.findarticles.com (accessed June 2, 2008).

5. Kevin Chappell, "Celeb Workout Secrets: You Can Have a Body Like the Stars," *Ebony*, November 1, 2008, www.highbeam.com (accessed November 3, 2008).

6. Quoted in "You Said It . . .," *Daily Post* (Liverpool, England), January 6, 2007, www.highbeam.com (accessed June 6, 2008).

7. "Small Business Telecom: Opportunities in the Women and Minority-owned Small Business Marketplace," 2000, Insight Research Corporation, www.insight-corp.com (accessed September 9, 2008).

8. Quoted by Anthony Asadullah Samad, "Between the Lines: 'Young B' and the New Women's Empowerment Movement," September 4, 2007, www.eurweb.com (accessed May 8, 2008).

9. Ibid.

10. Quoted by Kimberly Jade Norwood, "Blackthink's Acting White Stigma in Education and How It Fosters Academic Paralysis in Black Youth," *Howard Law Journal*, Spring 2007, //law.wustl.edu/Faculty/Documents/norwood/HowardActingWhite.pdf (accessed May 27, 2008).

11. Evelyn Nakano Glenn, "Yearning for Lightness: Transnational Circuits in the Marketing and Consumption of Skin Lighteners," *Gender & Society*, June 2008, www.socsci.mcmaster.ca (accessed September 20, 2008).

12. Quoted in "Your Race, Your Looks," www.glamour.com/magazine/2008/o2/race-beauty-panel (accessed January 16, 2009).

13. Ibid.

14. Sydney Dillard, "Is Black Beautiful? A Content Analysis of Beauty Characteristics of African-American Women in the Advertisements of *Cosmopolitan* and *Essence*," *McNair Scholars Journal*, 2005, www.siu.edu/mcnair (accessed May 8, 2008).

15. Mimi Valdes, "The Metamorphosis," *Vibe*, July 25, 2003, www.bookrags.com (accessed June 6, 2008).

16. Louise Archer, "The Impossibility of Girls' Educational 'Success': Entanglements of Gender, 'Race,' Class and Sexuality in the Production and Problematisation of Educational Femininities," Draft Working Paper for ESRC Seminar Series 'Girls in Education 3–16', *Cardiff* 24, November 2005, www.lancs.ac.uk (accessed June 11, 2008).

17. Art Sims, "Kelvyn Park H. S. Student Wins to 'Dream' with Disney," *Chicago Defender*, Jan. 9, 2008, www.newsbank.com (accessed June 6, 2008).

18. Quoted by Zetta Elliott, "Writing the Black (W)hole: Facing the Feminist Void," *Third Space*, January 2006, www.thirdspace.ca (accessed May 8, 2008).

19. Samantha C. Thrift, "Surviving Independent Women: Feminist Appropriations in the Cultural Production of Destiny's Child," Thesis at the University of Calgary, 2002, //dspace.ucalgary.ca (accessed May 8, 2008).

20. Daphne Brooks, "All That You Can't Leave Behind: Black Female Soul Singing and the Politics of Surrogation in the Age of Catastrophe," *Meridians: Feminism, Race, Transnationalism*, 2007, //muse.jhu.edu (accessed May 8, 2008).

21. Marie Connolly and Alan B. Krueger, "Rockonomics: The Economics of Popular Music," 2005, www.nber.org (accessed May 8, 2008).

22. "Pepsi Gladiator Ad to Be Launched in London," January 25, 2004, www.breaking.tcm.ie/entertainment (accessed September 9, 2008).

23. Ed Mayo," Shopping Generation," National Consumer Council, London, UK, 2005, www.ncc.org.uk (accessed May 8, 2008).

24. Quoted by John Wenzel, "More Than the Sum of Her Talents—a Brand," *Houston Chronicle*, August 20, 2007, 12.

25. Quoted by Lisa Hinojosa, "Dancer Doesn't Limit Herself to Just Ballet," December 9, 2007, www.caller.com (accessed May 8, 2008).

26. Sasha Frere-Jones, "Crazy for Love," *New Yorker*, September 25, 2006, www.newyorker.com (accessed November 3, 2008).

27. "Interview with Beyoncé," *CNN Larry King Live*, April 2, 2007, www.transcripts.cnn.com (accessed September 9, 2008).

Appendix 1

DISCOGRAPHY

ALBUMS

Destiny's Child

1998 *Destiny's Child*, Sony.
1999 *The Writing's on the Wall*, Sony.
2001 *Survivor*, Sony.
2001 *8 Days of Christmas*, Sony.
2002 *This Is the Remix*, Sony.
2004 *Destiny Fulfilled*, Sony.

Beyoncé

2003 *Dangerously in Love*, Sony.
2004 *Live at Wembley*, Sony.
2003 *Maximum Beyoncé*, Orchard.
2006 *B'Day*, Sony.
2006 *Beyoncé The Ultimate Performer*, Music World Entertainment.
2007 *The Beyoncé Experience Live!*, Sony.
2008 *I Am… Sasha Fierce*, Sony.

FILM SOUNDTRACKS

Destiny's Child

1997 "Killing Time," *Men in Black*

1998 "Get on the Bus," *Why Do Fools Fall in Love?*
1999 "Stimulate Me" (with Mocha), *Life*
2000 "Independent Women, Part I" and "DOT," *Charlie's Angels*
2000 "Perfect Man," *Romeo Must Die*
2000 "Big Momma's Theme"(with Da Brat and Vita), *Big Momma's House*

Solo

1999 "After All Is Said and Done" (with Marc Nelson), *The Best Man*
2000 "I Got That (with Amil)," *All Money Is Legal*
2002 "Keep Giving Your Love to Me," *Bad Boys 2*
2002 "Work It Out," *Austin Powers in Goldmember*
2002 "03 Bonnie & Clyde" (with Jay-Z), *The Blueprint–The Gift & the Curse*
2003 "Fighting Temptation" (with Missy Elliott, MC Lyte, and Free), *The Fighting Temptations*
2003 "Summertime" (with Ghostface Killah), *The Fighting Temptations*
2003 "Baby Boy" (with Sean Paul), Columbia, released as a single from *Dangerously in Love* album
2003 "Crazy in Love," single released by Sbme Import
2004 "Star Spangled Banner," Super Bowl XXXVIII, single released by Sony
2006 "Check on It" (with Slim thug), single released by Sony
2006 "Déjà vu" (featuring Jay-Z), single released by Columbia
2006 "Irreplaceable," single released by Sony
2007 "Beautiful Liar" (with Shakira), single released by Columbia Europe

VIDEOS

Destiny's Child

1999 "Bills, Bills, Bills"
2000 "Say My Name"
2000 "Jumpin' Jumpin'"
2000 "Independent Women, Part 1"
2001 "Survivor"
2001 "Bootylicious"
2001 "Emotion"
2002 "No, No, No"
2004 "Lose My Breath"

2004 "Soldier"
2005 "Girl"
2005 "Cater 2 U"
2005 "Stand Up for Love"

Beyoncé

2002 "Bonnie & Clyde"
2003 "Crazy Love"
2003 "Baby Boy"
2003 "Me, Myself and I"
2005 "Check On It"
2005 "Déjà Vu"
2006 "Listen"
2006 "Irreplaceable"
2006 "Ring the Alarm"
2007 "Beautiful Liar"
2007 "Upgrade U"
2007 "Suga Mama"
2007 "Freakum Dress"
2007 "Kitty Kat"
2007 "Flaws and All"
2007 "Green Light"
2007 "Get Me Bodied"
2008 "Halo"
2008 "If I Were a Boy"
2008 "Single Ladies (Put a Ring on It)"

FILMS

2001 *Carmen: A Hip Hopera*
2002 *Austin Powers in Goldmember*
2003 *The Fighting Temptations*
2006 *Fade to Black*
2006 *The Pink Panther*
2006 *Dreamgirls*

Appendix 2

AWARDS

DESTINY'S CHILD OR BEYONCÉ

1998

Soul Train Lady of Soul Awards

Best R&B/Soul Single by a Group, Band, or Duo ("No, No, No")
Best R&B/Soul or Rap New Artist ("No, No, No")
Best R&B/Soul Album of the Year by a Group, Band, or Duo (*Destiny's Child*)

2000

MTV Video Music Award, Best R&B Video ("Say My Name")

Billboard Music Awards

Top Pop Artist
Top Pop Artist, Duo or Group
Top Hot 100 Artists
Top Hot 100 Artists, Duo or Group
Top Hot Dance Maxi-Single Sales Artist ("Independent Women Part 1")
Top Hot Dance Maxi-Single Sales Artist, Duo or Group ("Independent Women Part 1")

Grammy Awards

Best R&B Vocal Performance by a Duo or Group ("Say My Name")
Best R&B Song ("Say My Name"—writers)

Soul Train Lady of Soul Awards

Best R&B/Soul Single by a Group, Band, or Duo ("Say My Name")
R&B/Soul Album of the Year by a Group, Band, or Duo (*The Writing's on the Wall*).
Direct Artist Award for Favorite Urban/Hip-Hop Group

2001

American Music Award for Favorite Soul/R&B by a Band, Duo or Group
ASCAP Pop Music Award, Songwriter of the Year
BET Award for Best Group
Grammy Award for Best R&B Vocal Performance by a Duo or Group ("Survivor")
MTV Video Music Award for Best R&B Video ("Survivor")
NAACP Image Award for Outstanding Duo or Group
Sammy Davis Jr. Award for Entertainer of the Year at the Soul Train Music Awards
Soul Train Lady of Soul Award for Best R&B/Soul Single by a Group, Band or Duo ("Survivor")
Teen Choice Award for Choice Pop Group
VH1/Vogue Fashion Award for Outrageous Group

Billboard Music Awards

Top Hot 100 Artists
Top Hot 100—Duo or Group
Top Hot Dance Maxi-Single Sales Artist
Top Hot Dance Maxi-Single Sales ("Independent Woman Part 1")
Top Hot Top 40 Artist
Top Pop Artist
Top Pop Artist—Duo or Group
Singles Artist of the Year
Group/Duo of the Year

Blockbuster Entertainment Awards

Favorite Group
Favorite Group-R&B

BMI Pop Awards

Most Performed Song ("Bills, Bills, Bills")
Most Performed Song ("Say My Name")

Radio Music Awards

Artist of the Year—Hip-Hop Rhythmic Radio
Artist of the Year—Top 40 Pop Radio

2002

Brit Award for Best International Group
Nickelodeon Kids' Choice Award for Favorite Singing Group

American Music Awards

Favorite Pop/Rock Album (Survivor)
Favorite Soul/R&B Band, Duo or Group

Soul Train Lady of Soul Awards

Best R&B/Soul Single by a Group, Band or Duo ("Emotion")
R&B /Soul Album of the Year by a Group, Band or Duo (*Survivor*)

World Music Awards

World's Best-selling Artist or Group
World's Best-selling Pop Group
World's Best-selling R&B Group

2003

VH1's Big Entertainer
Vibe Award for Coolest Collaboration along with Jay-Z for "Crazy in
    Love"

Billboard Music Awards

Hot 100 Award for Most Weeks at No. 1
Hot 100 Singles Artist-Female
New R&B/Hip-Hop Artist

MTV Europe Awards

Best Female Performer and Best R&B Artist (critics)
Best R&B Artist by readers of *Rolling Stone* magazine
Best R&B Award
Best Song of the Year ("Crazy in Love")

MTV Europe Music Awards

Best R&B Artists
Best Song of the Year ("Crazy in Love")

MTV Video Music Awards

Best Female Video ("Crazy in Love")
Best R&B Video ("Crazy in Love")
Best Choreography ("Crazy in Love")

2004

Billboard Music Award for Artistic Achievement
Brit Award for Best International Female Solo Artist
MTV Video Music Award for Best Female Video ("Naughty Girl")
NAACP Image Award for Entertainer of the Year
People's Choice Award for Favorite Female Performer
Radio Music Award for Artist of the Year-Top 40 Radio
Sammy Davis, Jr. Award for Entertainer of the Year-Female
Soul Train Music Award for R&B/Soul Album-Female (*Dangerously* in
      Love)
TRL First Lady Award

BET Awards

Best Female R&B Artist
Best Collaboration ("Crazy in Love")

Grammy Awards (Solo Awards)

Best R&B Vocal Performance-Female (*Dangerously in Love*)
Best R&B Vocal Performance by a Duo or Group ("The Closer I Get to
    You" with Luther Vandross)
Best Contemporary R&B Album (*Dangerously in Love*)
Best R&B Song ("Crazy in Love" with other artists)
Best Rap/Sung Collaboration ("Crazy in Love" with Jay-Z)

2005

Music Factory Award for Best International Group
NAACP Image Award for Outstanding Duo or Group
Soul Train Music Award for R&B/Soul Album by a Group, Band or Duo
    (*Destiny Fulfilled*)
TRL Award for Best Entrance

2006

Beyoncé, Kelly Rowland, and Michelle Williams received a star on
    Hollywood's Walk of Fame in Los Angeles.
Grammy Award for Best R&B Performance by a Duo with Vocals for "So
    Amazing" with Stevie Wonder
MTV Video Award for Best R&B Video for "Check on It" with Slim
    Thug

2007

American Music Award
ASCAP Pop Music Awards
Broadcast Film Critics Association Award (Critics Choice Award)
Grammy, Best Album of the Year: *B'Day*
International Star of the Year
Most Performed Song: "Check On It"
Most Performed Song: "Grillz"
MTV Video Music Award for Best Collaboration
Soul Train Music Award

BET Award

Best R&B Female Artist
Best R&B/Soul Single/Female for "Irreplaceable"
Best Song: "Listen" from the movie *Dreamgirls*
Best Video ("Irreplaceable")

Nickelodeon Kids' Choice Awards

Favorite Female Singer
Favorite Song: "Irreplaceable"

VH1 Soul Vibe Awards

R&B Artist of the Year
VStyle Award

Appendix 3

ALBUM REVIEWS

B'DAY

http://www.msnbc.msn.com/id/14717054/.
http://www.pitchforkmedia.com/article/record_review/38328-bday.

CARMEN: A HIP-HOPERA

http://www.phatmag.com/Mag%20Pages/Reviews/10_06_01/Carmen.
   html.

DANGEROUSLY IN LOVE

http://www.rollingstone.com/artists/beyoncé/albums/album/291273/
   review/6209670/dangerously_in_love.
http://www.shakingthrough.net/music/reviews/2003/beyoncé_
   dangerously_in_love_2003.html.

DESTINY FULFILLED

http://music.msn.com/album/?album=39803696.

DESTINY'S CHILD

http://www.billboard.com/bbcom/discography/index.jsp?JSESSIONID=C
WPDH75fvtMhfwzYjYhSprMy52FgnyN3jTt2l4PWYpgZn4MCJ3
0v!87636624&pid=248498&aid=281764.
http://musicmp3.ru/review_destinys-child__1s.html.

8 DAYS OF CHRISTMAS

http://www.rollingstone.com/artists/destinyschild/albums/album/195282/
review/5943810/8_days_of_christmas.

I AM ... SASHA FIERCE

www.rollingstone.com/reviews/album/24165028/review/24196171/
Iamsasha_fierce
http://entertainment.timesonline.co.uk/tol/arts_and_entertainment/
music/cd_reviews/article5199262.ece

SURVIVOR

http://www.metacritic.com/music/artists/destinyschild/survivor.
http://www.ffwdmag.com/cddestinyschild.htm.

THE BEYONCÉ EXPERIENCE

http://www.ravemagazine.com.au/content/view/3353/82/.

WRITING'S ON THE WALL

http://music.barnesandnoble.com/The-Writings-on-the-Wall/Destinys
Child/e/074646987025.
http://www.goldlyrics.com/review/destiny_s_child/writing_s_on_the_
wall/248332_destiny_s_child_second_album/.

SELECTED BIBLIOGRAPHY

BOOKS ABOUT BEYONCÉ

Dougherty, Terri. *Beyoncé*. Detroit: Lucent Books, 2007.

Dylan, Penelope. *Beyoncé*. New York: Rosen Books, 2007.

Hodgson, Nicola. *Beyoncé Knowles*. Chicago: Raintree, 2006.

Holt, Julia. *Beyoncé*. London: Hodder Murray, 2005.

Horn, Geoffrey M. *Beyoncé*. Milwaukee, WI: G. Stevens Publications, 2006.

O'Mara, Molly. *Beyoncé*. New York: PowerKids Press, 2007.

Patrick, Chris. *Beyoncé & Destiny's Child*. New York: Scholastic, 2005.

Tracy, Kathleen. *Beyoncé*. Hockessin, DE: Mitchell Lane Publishers, 2005.

Waters, Rosa. *Beyoncé*. Broomall, PA: Mason Crest Publishers, 2007.

Webster, Christine. *Beyoncé Knowles*. New York: Weigl Publishers, 2006.

BOOKS BY BEYONCÉ

Soul Survivors: The Official Autobiography of Destiny's Child. New York: Regan Books/HarperCollins, 2002.

ARTICLES ABOUT BEYONCÉ

Dunn, Jancee. "A Date with Destiny." *Rolling Stone*, May 24, 2001, www.find.galegroup.com.

Jones, Vanessa E. "Bewitched, Bothered, Beyoncé." *Boston Globe*, August 5, 2007, www.newsbank.com.

Norment, Lynn. "The Untold Story of How Tina and Mathew Knowles Created the Destiny's Child Gold Mine—Interview." *Ebony*, September 2001, www.findarticles.com.

Rotchford, Lesley. "Fun Fearless Female of the Year." *Cosmopolitan*, February 2006, 36–40.

Samuels, Allison. "What Beyoncé Wants." *Newsweek*, July 29, 2002, 52–53.

Toure. "Cover Story: A Woman Possessed." *Rolling Stone*, March 4, 2004, www.find.galegroup.com.

Valdes, Mimi. "The Metamorphosis." *Vibe*, July 25, 2003, www.bookrags.com.

Wartofsky, Alona. "A Child of Destiny—Beyoncé Knowles Is Growing into a Renaissance Woman." *Washington Post*, September 23, 2003, C01.

BOOKS ON RAP/HIP-HOP, CELEBRITY CULTURE, AND FEMINISM

Cashmore, Ellis. *Celebrity/Culture*. London: Routledge, 2006.

Darby, Derrick, and Tommie Shelby, eds. *Hip-Hop and Philosophy: Rhyme 2 Reason*. Chicago: Open Court, 2005.

Morgan-Murray, Joan. *When Chickenheads Come Home to Roost: A Hip-Hop Feminist Breaks It Down*. New York: Simon & Schuster, 2000.

Orth, Maureen. *The Importance of Being Famous: Behind the Scenes of the Celebrity Industrial Complex*. New York: Henry Holt, 2004.

Pough, Gwendolyn D. *Check It While I Wreck It: Black Womanhood, Hip-Hop Culture and the Public Sphere*. Boston: Northeastern, 2004.

Vibe Magazine. *Hip-Hop Divas*. New York: Three Rivers Press, 2001.

INTERNET

"Beyoncé Knowles—Beyoncé Thrilled by First Dance Teacher." June 9, 2006, www.contactmusic.com.

"Beyoncé: The Ice Princess." *Blender*, October 2006, www.blender.com.

Beyoncé's Official Web Site, www.beyoncéonline.com.

Cox, Tony. "Mathew Knowles on Fatherhood and *Beyoncé*." November 27, 2006, www.npr.org.

Johnson, Billy. "Destiny Awaits." May 27, 2004, www.music.yahoo.com.

Tyrangiel, Josh. "Destiny's Adult." *Time*, June 30, 2003, www.time.com.

Warner, Roberts. "Tina Knowles: Pop Star's Mom Sews Some Diva-licious Threads." September 2007, www.htexas.com.

INDEX

About the Author

JANICE ARENOFSKY is a professional writer.